TEACHER'S PET PUBLICATIONS

LITPLAN TEACHER PACK
for
Letters From Rifka
based on the book by
Karen Hesse

Written by
Barbara M. Linde, MA Ed.

© 2006 Teacher's Pet Publications
All Rights Reserved

The Lit Plan on *Letters from Rifka* has been brought to you
by Teacher's Pet Publications, Inc.

Copyright Teacher's Pet Publications 2006
All Rights Reserved

Only the student materials in this unit plan may be reproduced.
Pages such as worksheets and study guides may be reproduced for use in the purchaser's classroom.

For any additional copyright questions, contact Teacher's Pet Publications.

www.tpet.com

TABLE OF CONTENTS *Letters from Rifka*

Introduction	6
Unit Objectives	9
Reading Assignment Sheet	10
Unit Outline	11
Study Questions	15
Quiz/Study Questions (Multiple Choice)	26
Pre-Reading Vocabulary Worksheets	43
Lesson One (Introductory Lesson)	59
Nonfiction Assignment Sheet	65
Oral Reading Evaluation Form	70
Writing Assignment 1	72
Writing Evaluation Form	73
Writing Assignment 2	81
Extra Writing Assignments/ Discussion Questions	83
Quotations	84
Writing Assignment 3	88
Vocabulary Review Activities	89
Unit Review Activities	91
Unit Tests	99
Unit Resource Materials	139
Vocabulary Resource Materials	159

A FEW NOTES ABOUT THE AUTHOR
Karen Hesse

HESSE, Karen (August 29, 1952–) Karen Hesse was born and grew up in Baltimore, Maryland. As a child, she often wrote in her journals. Her fifth grade teacher encouraged her writing and gave Hesse the idea that she could one day become a professional writer. In 1975 she graduated from the University of Maryland. While there, she studied theater, anthropology, psychology, and English.

In 1976 Hesse and her husband settled in Brattleboro, Vermont, where they still live. She joined a writing group and had various jobs including waitress, nanny, librarian, book reviewer, and proofreader. She also raised two daughters.

Hesse's books have won many awards. Her first book, *Wish on a Unicorn*, was published in 1991 and The Hungry Mind Review selected it as a Children's Book of Distinction. *Letters from Rifka*, her second book, won a Christopher Medal and was chosen by the American Library Association as a Best Book for Young Adults. It was also named an ALA Notable Children's Book and a School Library Journal Best Book of the Year. *Sable* was also chosen as a School Library Journal Best Book of the Year. *Phoenix Rising* was cited as an ALA Best Book for Young Adults, an ALA Notable Children's Book, and an SLJ Best Book. *The Music of Dolphins* was chosen as an ALA Best Book for Young Adults. *Out of the Dust* won the Newbery Medal and the Scott O'Dell Award in 1998, and was also named an ALA Best Book for Young Adults, an ALA Notable Children's Book. It won honors from Publishers Weekly, the School-Library Journal, and Booklist.

Hesse credits her writers group for encouraging her to expand a draft of a picture book into the full-length novel *Out of the Dust*. She does extensive research for all of her books. She has been a member and leader of the Southern Vermont chapter of the Society of Children's Writers and Illustrators.

In 2002 Hesse received the prestigious MacArthur Fellowship award, which is often called "the genius award." According to the School and Library Journal, the Foundation praised Hesse for "expanding the possibilities of literature for children and young adults." Her books have been translated into Spanish, French, and German.

List of Hesse's Books:
- *Wish on a Unicorn*, 1991
- *Letters from Rifka*, 1992
- *Lavender* 1993
- *Poppy's Chair*, 1993
- *Lester's Dog*, 1993
- *Phoenix Rising*, 1994
- *Sable*, 1994
- *A Time of Angels*, 1995
- *The Music of Dolphins*, 1996
- *Out of the Dust*, 1997
- *Just Juice*, 1998
- *Come On, Rain!* 1999
- *A Time of Angels*, 2000
- *Witness*, 2001
- *Young Nick's Head*, 2001
- *A Civil War Diary of Amelia Martin*, 2002
- *Stowaway*, 2003
- *Aleutian Sparrow*, 2003
- *The Cats in Krasinski Square*, 2004

INTRODUCTION *Letters from Rifka*

This unit has been designed to develop students' reading, writing, thinking, listening, and speaking skills through exercises and activities related to *Letters from Rifka* by Karen Hesse. It includes twenty lessons, supported by extra resource materials.

The **introductory lesson** introduces students to *Letters from Rifka*. Following the introductory activity, students are given an explanation of how the activity relates to the book they are about to read. Following the transition, students are given the materials they will be using during the unit. They are also introduced to the nonfiction assignment. At the end of the lesson, students begin the pre-reading work for the first reading assignment.

The **reading assignments** are approximately 25 pages each; some are a little shorter while others are a little longer. Students have approximately 15 minutes of pre-reading work to do prior to each reading assignment. This pre-reading work involves reviewing the study questions for the assignment and doing some vocabulary work for 9 to 10 vocabulary words they will encounter in their reading.

The **study guide questions** are fact-based questions; students can find the answers to these questions right in the text. These questions come in two formats: short answer or multiple choice. The best use of these materials is probably to use the short answer version of the questions as study guides for students (since answers will be more complete), and to use the multiple-choice version for occasional quizzes. It might be a good idea to make transparencies of your answer keys for the overhead projector.

The **vocabulary work** is intended to enrich students' vocabularies as well as to aid in the students' understanding of the book. Prior to each reading assignment, students will complete a two-part worksheet for approximately 9 to 10 vocabulary words in the upcoming reading assignment. Part I focuses on students' use of general knowledge and contextual clues by giving the sentence in which the word appears in the text. Students are then to write down what they think the words mean based on the words' usage. Part II gives students dictionary definitions of the words and has them match the words to the correct definitions based on the words' contextual usage. Students should then have an understanding of the words when they meet them in the text.

After each reading assignment, students will go back and formulate answers for the study guide questions. Discussion of these questions serves as a review of the most important events and ideas presented in the reading assignments.

After students complete extra discussion questions, there is a vocabulary review lesson which pulls together all of the separate vocabulary lists for the reading assignments and gives students a review of all of the words they have studied.

Following the reading of the book, a lesson is devoted to the **extra discussion questions/writing assignments**. These questions focus on interpretation, critical analysis and personal response, employing a variety of thinking skills and adding to the students' understanding of the novel. These questions are done as a **group activity**.

Using the information they have acquired so far through individual work and class discussions, students get together to further examine the text and to brainstorm ideas relating to the themes of the novel.

The group activity is followed by a **reports and discussion** session in which the groups share their ideas about the book with the entire class; thus, the entire class gets exposed to many different ideas regarding the themes and events of the book.

There are **three writing assignments** in this unit, each with the purpose of informing, persuading, or having students express personal opinions. The first assignment is to **express personal opinions**. Students write from the point of view of Rifka and explain why she wants to go to America. The second writing assignment is to **inform**. Students write a series of travel tips to share with other students. The third writing assignment is to **persuade**. Students write from the point of view of Rifka and persuade someone back home to immigrate to America.

In addition, there is a **nonfiction reading assignment**. Students are required to read a piece of nonfiction related in some way to *Letters from Rifka*. After reading their nonfiction pieces, students will fill out a worksheet on which they answer questions regarding facts, interpretation, criticism, and personal opinions. During one class period, students make oral presentations about the nonfiction pieces they have read. This not only exposes all students to a wealth of information; it also gives students the opportunity to practice public speaking.

The **review lesson** pulls together all of the aspects of the unit. The teacher is given four or five choices of activities or games to use which all serve the same basic function of reviewing all of the information presented in the unit.

The **unit test** comes in two formats: all multiple choice matching true/false or with a mixture of matching, short answer, and composition. As a convenience, two different tests for each format have been included.

There are additional **support materials** included with this unit. The **resource materials sections** include suggestions for an in-class library, crossword and word search puzzles related to the novel, and extra vocabulary worksheets. There is a list of **bulletin board ideas** which gives the teacher suggestions for bulletin boards to go along with this unit. In addition, there is a list of extra class activities the teacher could choose from to enhance the unit or as a substitution for an exercise the teacher might feel is inappropriate for his/her class. Answer keys are located directly after the reproducible student materials throughout the unit.

UNIT PLAN ADAPTATIONS – *Letters from Rifka*

Block Schedule

Depending on the length of your class periods, and the frequency with which the class meets, you may wish to choose one of the following options:
- Complete two of the daily lessons in one class period.
- Have students complete all reading and writing activities in class.
- Assign all reading to be completed out of class, and concentrate on the worksheets and discussions in class.
- Assign the projects from the daily lessons at the beginning of the unit, and allow time each day for students to work on them.
- Use some of the Unit and Vocabulary Resource activities during every class.

Gifted & Talented / Advanced Classes
- Emphasize the projects and the extra discussion questions.
- Have students complete all of the writing activities.
- Assign the reading to be completed out of class and focus on the discussions in class.
- Encourage students to develop their own questions.

ESL / ELD
- Assign a partner to help the student read the text aloud.
- Tape record the text and have the student listen and follow along in the text.
- Give the student the study guide worksheets to use as they read.
- Provide pictures and demonstrations to explain difficult vocabulary words and concepts.
- Conduct guided reading lessons, asking students to stop frequently and explain what they have read.
- Show the movie version of the novel and help students identify characters and events, and relate the action in their own words. You may want to show the movie without the sound and explain the actions in your own words.

UNIT OBJECTIVES – *Letters from Rifka*

1. Through reading *Letters from Rifka* students will analyze characters and their situations to better understand the themes of the novel.

2. Students will analyze the setting and discuss its importance in the novel.

3. Students will demonstrate their understanding of the text on four levels: factual, interpretive, critical, and personal.

4. Students will identify the sequence markers in the novel and discuss the importance of sequence in the novel.

5. Students will practice reading aloud and silently to improve their skills in each area.

6. Students will enrich their vocabularies and improve their understanding of the novel through the vocabulary lessons prepared for use in conjunction with it.

7. Students will answer questions to demonstrate their knowledge and understanding of the main events and characters in *Letters from Rifka*.

8. Students will practice writing through a variety of writing assignments.

9. The writing assignments in this are geared to several purposes:
    a. To check the students' reading comprehension
    b. To make students think about the ideas presented by the novel
    c. To make students put those ideas into perspective
    d. To encourage critical and logical thinking
    e. To provide the opportunity to practice good grammar and improve students' use of the English language.

10. Students will read aloud, report, and participate in large and small group discussions to improve their public speaking and personal interaction skills.

READING ASSIGNMENT SHEET Letters *from Rifka*

Date Assigned	Reading Assignment	Completion Date
	September 2, 1919, Russia through October 5, 1919, Motziv, Poland	
	November 3, 1919, Motziv, Poland through December 1, 1919, Warsaw, Poland	
	February 25, 1920, Antwerp, Belgium through September 14, 1920, Antwerp, Belgium	
	September 16, 1920, Somewhere on the Atlantic Ocean through October 7, 1920, Ellis Island	
	October 9, 1920, Ellis Island through October 11, 1920, Ellis Island	
	October 14, 1920, Ellis Island through October 22, 1920, Ellis Island	

WRITING ASSIGNMENT LOG Letters *from Rifka*

Date Assigned	Writing Assignment	Completion Date
	Writing Assignment 1	
	Writing Assignment 2	
	Writing Assignment 3	
	Non-fiction Assignment	

UNIT OUTLINE *Letters from Rifka*

1 Introduction	2 PVR Sept. 2, 1919, through Oct. 5, 1919 Nonfiction Assignment	3 Study?? Sept. 2, 1919, through Oct. 5, 1919 PVR Nov 3, 1919, through Dec. 1, 1919	4 Study?? Nov 3, 1919, through Dec. 1, 1919 Minilesson: Character Traits	5 Oral Reading Evaluation
6 Writing Assignment #1 Personal Opinion	7 PVR Study?? Feb. 25, 1920, through Sept. 14, 1920, Minilesson: Setting	8 PVR Study?? Sept. 16, 1920, through Oct. 7, 1920	9 Quiz Sept. 2, 1919 through Oct. 7, 1920 Writing Conference	10 PVR Oct. 9, 1920, through Oct. 11, 1920
11 Study?? Oct. 9, 1920, through Oct. 11, 1920 Minilesson: Sequence	12 Writing Assignment #2 Inform	13 PVR Study?? Oct. 14, 1920, through Oct. 22, 1920	14 Extra Writing/Discussion Questions	15 Quotations
16 Writing Assignment #3 Persuade	17 Vocabulary Review	18 Unit Review	19 Test	20 Nonfiction Assignment

Key: P = Preview Study Questions   V=Vocabulary Work   R= Read

STUDY GUIDE QUESTIONS

SHORT ANSWER STUDY GUIDE QUESTIONS *Letters from Rifka*

September 2, 1919, Russia through October 5, 1919, Motziv, Poland
1. To whom is Rifka writing, and where is this person?
2. Where are Rifka and her family going, and how do they plan to get there?
3. Why is the family going on this journey?
4. What gift does Rifka have with her, and who gave it to her?
5. What is Rifka's job as the family is getting ready to go, and why does she have to do this?
6. How does Rifka go about doing her job, and who helps her?
7. Describe the family's treatment at the Polish border. How does Rifka react to this?
8. What is missing when Rifka gets her rucksack back? What is Mama's response?
9. How is Uncle Avrum's family different from Rifka's family?
10. Why is the family stuck in Motziv, Poland?

November 3, 1919, Motziv, Poland through December 1, 1919, Warsaw, Poland
1. What does Rifka try to do for Saul, and what is the result?
2. What does Rifka learn when she visits her mother in the hospital in Motziv?
3. How many of Rifka's family members survive their typhus illnesses?
4. Where do they go when they leave Motziv? Why do they go there?
5. What are the names of Rifka's older brothers? How long ago did they leave home? Has Rifka ever met them?
6. Describe Rifka's meeting with the peasant girl on the train. Include what the girl looked like, the language she spoke, and what Rifka did for her.
7. What does the doctor at the steamship say about Rifka? What does Rifka realize when he says this?
8. What is the HIAS? How does it help Rifka and her family?
9. What is Rifka's response to the worker's suggestion? What is her father's response?
10. What does Rifka do? How does she describe herself?

February 25, 1920, Antwerp, Belgium through September 14, 1920, Antwerp, Belgium
1. What do Mama and Papa give Rifka just before they part?
2. What does Rifka do to celebrate her thirteenth birthday?
3. What does Rifka learn from Sister Katrina?
4. What compliment does Sister Katrina give Rifka? What is Rifka's thought about the compliment that she writes to Tovah?
5. What does Sister Katrina tell Rifka to do? Why does Sister Katrina think this is a good idea? What is Rifka's answer? What does Rifka do?
6. What does Rifka wonder about herself now?
7. What does Rifka do when she gets lost in Antwerp? Who helps her? What does she think of this person? What does she think about this experience?
8. What does Rifka think of Antwerp? Include her thoughts about the people, the scenery, and the food. What foods does she discover and what does she think of them?
9. What does Rifka buy for herself? Why is this purchase important?
10. What good news does Rifka receive? What concern does she still have?

Short Answer Study Guide Questions *Letters from Rifka*

September 16, 1920, Somewhere on the Atlantic Ocean
through October 7, 1920, Ellis Island
1. Whom does Rifka meet on the ship and what is their relationship like?
2. Briefly describe the storm at sea. Tell what Rifka does and how she feels. Tell how long the storm lasts.
3. What happens to Pieter during the storm? How does Rifka feel about it?
4. Describe what Rifka does after the storm is over and after she finds out about Pieter. Include how she feels.
5. How does Rifka describe what America meant to her in Russia? How does she describe what it means as she is sailing into New York?
6. What does Rifka see as the ship comes into New York Harbor? How does she describe this?
7. What do the doctors on Ellis Island tell Rifka and her family? How do they all take this news?
8. Explain what the doctors mean when they tell Rifka the American government may view her as a "social responsibility." Include her response.
9. Describe the jobs Rifka does at the hospital.
10. Why does Rifka dislike Ilya at first? Why does she feed Ilya? How does she feel about her actions?

October 9, 1920, Ellis Island through October 11, 1920, Ellis Island
1. What gift does Saul bring for Rifka? Why is he surprised that she recognizes it? What does she tell him about this gift?
2. What else about Rifka surprises Saul? What does Rifka tell him about this?
3. Saul asks what he should tell their mother about Rifka's hair. What is her reply?
4. What happens while Ilya and Saul are struggling over the Pushkin book? How does Ilya react to this?
5. What does Saul say about Ilya? What does he say about the Pushkin book?
6. As Saul and Rifka are quarreling, she remembers something that someone told her. This calms her down. What does she remember, and who said it?
7. Describe what each of the Nebrot family members is doing for work in New York.
8. Rifka gives Saul the money she did not spend in Antwerp. What does she tell him to do with it?
9. When Mama visits the hospital, she watches Rifka doing her jobs. What does she say about this?
10. What does Rifka want to help Ilya to do? Why?

Short Answer Study Guide Questions *Letters from Rifka*

October 14, 1920, Ellis Island through October 22, 1920, Ellis Island
1. What "trouble" do Ilya and Rifka get into? Why is Rifka frightened? What is Nurse Bowen's response when Rifka tells her about it?
2. What does Rifka ask Nurse Bowen to give her? What does she do with it? How does she feel about it?
3. What is happening to Rifka's head? What does she fear?
4. What does Rifka realize when she thinks about going back to Berdichev?
5. At the hearing, Rifka tells Ilya's uncle that Ilya is afraid of him. What is his uncle's response? How does this response change Ilya's actions?
6. What is the result of Ilya's actions?
7. What action does Ilya take that helps with Mr. Fargate's decision about Rifka entering the United States?
8. What does Rifka discover when her kerchief falls off at the hearing?
9. Saul tells Rifka there are gifts waiting at home. What are they?
10. How will the family get back to their home from the hospital?

Answer Key Short Answer Study Guide Questions *Letters from Rifka*

<u>September 2, 1919, Russia through October 5, 1919, Motziv, Poland</u>
1. To whom is Rifka writing, and where is this person?
    Rifka is writing to her cousin Tovah. Tovah is still living in Berdichev, Russia.

2. Where are Rifka and her family going, how do they plan to get there?
    They are planning to leave Russia by train, go into Poland, and from there they want to go to America.

3. Why is the family going on this journey?
    Rifka's older brother Nathan has already been taken into the Russian army and now her brother Saul is about to be taken. Rifka's parents have planned for this time to escape and live with their older sons, who have already moved to America.

4. What gift does Rifka have with her, and who gave it to her?
    She has a copy of a book of poetry by a Russian poet named Pushkin. Her cousin Tovah gave it to her.

5. What is Rifka's job as the family is getting ready to go and why does she have to do this?
    Rifka distracts the guards at the train station so they don't search the boxcars and find her other family members. She is the only one in the family with blond hair, so she looks Russian. She also speaks Russian without a Yiddish accent.

6. How does she go about doing her job, and who helps her?
    She talks to the guards and has mostly distracted them. Her Uncle Avrum asks them for help, saying someone has broken into his factory. Since Avrum is a respected businessman, the guards have to help him. They go with him and the train leaves.

7. Describe the family's treatment at the Polish border. How does Rifka react to this?
    The family is ordered to get off the train at the border. Guards search them and order them to remove their clothes so the doctor can check them for diseases. Their bodies, clothes, and possessions are fumigated. Rifka says the doctor made her feel dirty.

8. What is missing when Rifka gets her rucksack back? What is Mama's response?
    Someone has taken Mama's candlesticks from Rifka's rucksack. Mama says it could have been worse and tells Rifka to stop sniffling and get dressed.

9. How is Uncle Avrum's family different from Rifka's family?
    Uncle Avrum's family has money. They are treated better and can travel around the country. Rifka's family is poor, so they are treated more like criminals.

Answer Key Short Answer Study Guide Questions *Letters from Rifka*

<u>September 2, 1919, Russia through October 5, 1919, Motziv, Poland, continued</u>
10. Why is the family stuck in Motziv, Poland?
    Rifka gets sick with typhus. It is several weeks before she feels better. Her mother, father, and Nathan also get sick. They are taken to a hospital and leave her in Saul's care.

<u>November 3, 1919, Motziv, Poland through December 1, 1919, Warsaw, Poland</u>
1. What does Rifka try to do for Saul, and what is the result?
   She saves part of her breakfast roll for him. The daughter of the innkeeper spies on Rifka, finds the roll, and eats it.

2. What does Rifka learn when she visits her mother in the hospital in Motziv?
   Rifka begins to understand the Polish language.

3. How many of Rifka's family members survive their typhus illnesses?
   They all survive.

4. Where do they go when they leave Motziv? Why do they go there?
   They go to Warsaw, Poland. They get the money the older brothers have sent and plan to buy steamship tickets.

5. What are the names of Rifka's older brothers? How long ago did they leave home? Has Rifka ever met them?
   They are Isaac, Reuben, and Asher. They left home fourteen years ago. She has never met them because they left home before Rifka was born.

6. Describe Rifka's meeting with the peasant girl on the train. Include what the girl looked like, the language she spoke, and what Rifka did for her.
   The girl was about sixteen and spoke Polish. She was nursing a little baby. She had oily hair with sores on her scalp. Rifka offered to braid the girl's hair and she accepted.

7. What does the doctor at the steamship say about Rifka? What does Rifka realize when he says this?
   He says that Rifka has ringworm and cannot go on the ship. The treatment will take many months. Rifka realizes that the girl on the train had ringworm and that's where she got it.

Answer Key Short Answer Study Guide Questions *Letters from Rifka*

November 3, 1919, Motziv, Poland through December 1, 1919, Warsaw, Poland

8. What is the HIAS? How does it help Rifka and her family?
    The HIAS is the Hebrew Immigration Aid Society. They help Jews with immigration and other problems. One of the workers in Warsaw arranges for Rifka to go to Antwerp, Belgium and live with a family while she gets treatment at a hospital for the ringworm.

9. What is Rifka's response to the worker's suggestion? What is her father's response?
    She says she would rather go back to Berdichev. Her father reminds her that the Russians are angry at the family because her five brothers escaped service in the Army. If she goes back she will be killed.

10. What does Rifka do? How does she describe herself?
    Rifka agrees to go to Antwerp. She says she is like an orphan.

February 25, 1920, Antwerp, Belgium through September 14, 1920, Antwerp, Belgium

1. What do Mama and Papa give Rifka just before they part?
    Mama gives her the gold locket that Papa gave her as a wedding gift. Papa gives her his tallis, or prayer shawl.

2. What does Rifka do to celebrate her thirteenth birthday?
    She had a mitzvah for herself, celebrating becoming a woman. She made a Star of David from some broom straws, put on her father's prayer shawl, and said the Hebrew prayers she remembered.

3. What does Rifka learn from Sister Katrina?
    She learns to speak Flemish. She also learns how important cleanliness is in curing the ringworm. Sister Katrina teaches her a Catholic prayer to say when she wants to scratch her head.

4. What compliment does Sister Katrina give Rifka? What is Rifka's thought about the compliment that she writes to Tovah?
    Sister Katrina tells Rifka she is clever. Rifka writes that Tovah would like hearing that someone thinks she (Rifka) is clever.

5. What does Sister Katrina tell Rifka to do? Why does Sister Katrina think this is a good idea? What is Rifka's answer? What does Rifka do?
    Sister tells Rifka to get out and enjoy herself in Antwerp. She says that Rifka needs some good fresh air and exercise. At first Rifka says she is happy in her room; she does not need exercise, only to go to America. Then she does go out and explore the city.

Answer Key Short Answer Study Guide Questions *Letters from Rifka*

<u>February 25, 1920, Antwerp, Belgium through September 14, 1920, Antwerp, Belgium,</u> continued

6. What does Rifka wonder about herself now?
    Rifka is bald due to the ringworm and treatment. She wonders if she will stay bald. If so, she wonders if she will get a husband? She asks if Tovah will still love her.

7. What does Rifka do when she gets lost in Antwerp? Who helps her? What does she think of this person? What does she think about this experience?
    She asks a milkman for help. He walks her all the way home. He reminds her of her Uncle Zeb. His horse reminds her of her uncle's horse, Lotkeh. When she says goodbye to the milkman she feels like she is also finally saying goodbye to her uncle. She wonders how to repay someone for such kindness, and if her brothers would have helped someone like the milkman helped her.

8. What does Rifka think of Antwerp? Include her thoughts about the people, the scenery, and the food. What foods does she discover and what does she think of them?
    She thinks Antwerp is wonderful. The people are friendly and kind, the food is splendid, and the scenery is wonderful. She discovers ice cream and chocolate and thinks they are wonderful.

9. What does Rifka buy for herself? Why is this purchase important?
    She buys a hat. She can wear it to cover her bald head. The ringworm is clearing up, so she does not have to wear a kerchief all the time. She does not have to look like "a poor, needy immigrant Jew from Berdichev."

10. What good news does Rifka receive? What concern does she still have?
    The ringworm is cleared up and she is able to leave for America. However, she is still bald, which concerns her.

<u>September 16, 1920, Somewhere on the Atlantic Ocean</u>
<u>through October 7, 1920, Ellis Island</u>
1. Whom does Rifka meet on the ship, and what is their relationship like?
    She meets a young sailor named Pieter. They like each other. She says he is like a brother, but better.

2. Briefly describe the storm at sea. Tell what Rifka does and how she feels. Tell how long the storm lasts.
    The storm starts at night and the force of it throws her on the floor. She goes on deck, where she is sick. Pieter moves her away from the side of the ship. He saves her from being pulled overboard by a wave. Then he takes her to steerage to be safe. The passengers stay in steerage for thirty-six hours.

Answer Key Short Answer Study Guide Questions *Letters from Rifka*

3. What happens to Pieter during the storm? How does Rifka feel about it?
    He washes overboard. Rifka feels like she is smothering. She cannot see or hear.

4. Describe what Rifka does after the storm is over and after she finds out about Pieter. Include how she feels.
    Rifka cries until she cannot cry anymore. She feels how defenseless all people, not just Jews, are.

5. How does Rifka describe what America meant to her in Russia? How does she describe what it means as she is sailing into New York?
    In Russia she thinks America is excitement and adventure. Now it is a place to start over. She thinks life can be good in America for a clever girl.

6. What does Rifka see as the ship comes into New York Harbor? How does she describe this?
    She sees the Statue of Liberty, which she calls Miss Liberty. The statue is lifting a lamp to light the way for the immigrants.

7. What do the doctors on Ellis Island tell Rifka and her family? How do they all take this news?
    The doctors say that Rifka cannot enter the United States. They are keeping her in the hospital for contagious diseases. They want to make sure the ringworm has been cured, and they are concerned because she is still bald.

8. Explain what the doctors mean when they tell Rifka the American government may view her as a "social responsibility." Include her response.
    Since she is bald, she may never find a husband. Then the government will have to take care of her. Rifka says she does not need hair to be a good wife. Also, according to Jewish law a woman may shave her head. She thinks that in America, looks are more important than wits.

9. Describe the jobs Rifka does at the hospital.
    She has learned some English, so she translates for the Russian and Polish patients. She takes care of a baby girl who has typhus. She also takes care of a young Russian peasant boy named Ilya.

10. Why does Rifka dislike Ilya at first? Why does she feed Ilya? How does she feel about her actions?
    She dislikes him because he is a Russian peasant. If they were both in Russia, it would be his people killing hers. But she sees that he is just a scared little boy. She encourages him to eat and then feels very good about it.

Answer Key Short Answer Study Guide Questions *Letters from Rifka*

<u>October 9, 1920, Ellis Island through October 11, 1920, Ellis Island</u>
1. What gift does Saul bring for Rifka? Why is he surprised that she recognizes it? What does she tell him about this gift?
    He brings her a banana. He is surprised that she knows how to peel it because they didn't have bananas in Russia. She tells him she had bananas in Antwerp.

2. What else about Rifka surprises Saul? What does Rifka tell him about this?
    He is surprised that she knows as much English as she does, since she has only been in America for nine days. She tells him that Nurse Bowen and Doctor Askin help her learn English and she also learned some in Antwerp.

3. Saul asks what he should tell their mother about Rifka's hair. What is her reply?
    She says to tell the truth, that she is bald and her hair has not grown back after a year.

4. What happens while Ilya and Saul are struggling over the Pushkin book? How does Ilya react to this?
    The Star of David falls onto the floor and breaks. Ilya runs out of the ward.

5. What does Saul say about Ilya? What does he say about the Pushkin book?
    He says Ilya is a "nasty little peasant." Rifka should not be associating with him. He tells her to throw away the Pushkin book.

6. As Saul and Rifka are quarreling, she remembers something that someone told her. This calms her down. What does she remember, and who said it?
    She remembers that Pieter told her she was a treasure to her family. She stops quarreling and asks Saul to tell her about the family.

7. Describe what each of the Nebrot family members is doing for work in New York.
    Mama and Papa are working in a clothing factory. Nathan works in a bakery. Saul goes to school. Isaac married a girl named Sadie Chenowitz, whose family is also from Berdichev. They have a baby boy named Aaron.

8. Rifka gives Saul the money she did not spend in Antwerp. What does she tell him to do with it?
    She tells him to buy new candlesticks for their mother.

9. When Mama visits the hospital, she watches Rifka doing her jobs. What does she say about this?
    Mama says Rifka is like her father, who knows how to heal people. Mama also admires the way Rifka is learning English.

Answer Key Short Answer Study Guide Questions *Letters from Rifka*

October 9, 1920, Ellis Island through October 11, 1920, Ellis Island, continued

10. What does Rifka want to help Ilya to do? Why?
    She wants to help him see that his future is in staying in America, not in going back to Russia. The doctors think he is a simpleton because he does not talk or feed himself. She knows he is clever because he can read the Pushkin book.

October 14, 1920, Ellis Island through October 22, 1920, Ellis Island

1. What "trouble" do Ilya and Rifka get into? Why is Rifka frightened? What is Nurse Bowen's response when Rifka tells her about it?
    Ilya unrolls a roll of toilet paper. Rifka is upset because in Russia it is a crime to waste paper. She thinks they will get killed or sent back to Russia. Nurse Bowen laughs and says it is not a crime to waste paper in America. There is plenty of paper.

2. What does Rifka ask Nurse Bowen to give her? What does she do with it? How does she feel about it?
    She asks Nurse Bowen for some paper. She begins writing her own poems on the paper. She is happy to be writing. The writing comforts her. She thinks she is clever to be a poet.

3. What is happening to Rifka's head? What does she fear?
    Her head is itching. She is afraid to take off the kerchief and see the ringworm sores again. She is afraid if the doctors see the ringworm they will send her back to Russia.

4. What does Rifka realize when she thinks about going back to Berdichev?
    She realizes that she has seen too much of the world to ever go back there.

5. At the hearing, Rifka tells Ilya's uncle that Ilya is afraid of him. What is his uncle's response? How does this response change Ilya's actions?
    The uncle says he loves Ilya because he is the uncle's flesh and blood. He is working hard to have the money to bring Ilya to America. When Ilya hears that, he begins reading from the Pushkin book.

6. What is the result of Ilya's actions?
    Mr. Fargate, the doctor, the nurse and Ilya's uncle are amazed that he can read so well. Mr. Fargate approves his entry into America.

7. What action does Ilya take that helps with Mr. Fargate's decision about Rifka entering the United States?
    Ilya recites one of Rifka's poems from memory. Mr. Fargate is impressed and says she may enter the country.

Answer Key Short Answer Study Guide Questions *Letters from Rifka*

October 14, 1920, Ellis Island through October 22, 1920, Ellis Island
  8. What does Rifka discover when her kerchief falls off at the hearing?
      She discovers that she has some hair growing back.

  9. Saul tells Rifka there are gifts waiting at home. What are they?
      There are new candlesticks for Mama and paper for Rifka.

  10. How will the family get back to their home from the hospital?
      Isaac has gone to his home to get his car. He will drive them all to their home so Rifka can "enter America in style."

MULTIPLE CHOICE QUIZ/ STUDY GUIDE QUESTIONS *Letters from Rifka*

September 2, 1919, Russia through October 5, 1919, Motziv, Poland

1. Rifka is writing to Tovah. Who is Tovah?
    A. Tovah is Rifka's brother, who lives in New York City.
    B. Tovah is Rifka's uncle, who lives in Montreal, Canada.
    C. Tovah is Rifka's grandmother, who lives in Berlin, Germany.
    D. Tovah is Rifka's cousin who lives in Berdichev, Russia.

2. True or False: Rifka and her family are planning to go to America.
    A. True
    B. False

3. The family is going on this journey so _____.
    A. Rifka's father can search for gold in California
    B. Rifka can get a better education
    C. Rifka's brothers will not serve in the army
    D. Rifka's mother can get the surgery she needs

4. What gift from Tovah does Rifka have with her?
    A. a map of the United States
    B. a book of poetry by Pushkin
    C. a Russian/English dictionary
    D. a drawing of the two of them together

5. What is Rifka's job as the family is getting ready to go?
    A. Rifka distracts the guards at the train station.
    B. Rifka goes into town to buy food and other supplies.
    C. Rifka buys the train tickets.
    D. Rifka crawls through the cars looking for the best place to hide.

6. Who helps Rifka with her job as the family is getting ready to go?
    A. Tovah
    B. Uncle Avrum
    C. Asher
    D. her father

7. The treatment of the doctor at the Polish border makes Rifka feel _____.
    A. happy
    B. worried
    C. relieved
    D. dirty

Multiple Choice Quiz/ Study Guide Questions *Letters from Rifka*

<u>September 2, 1919, Russia through October 5, 1919, Motziv, Poland</u>
8. What is missing when Rifka gets her rucksack back?
    A. Rifka's book
    B. all of the family's money
    C. Mama's candlesticks
    D. Rifka's clothes

9. True or False: Uncle Avrum's family has money. They are treated better and can travel around the country.
    A. True
    B. False

10. Why is the family stuck in Motziv, Poland?
    A. They run out of money.
    B. Rifka gets sick with typhus.
    C. They are waiting for their illegal papers to come through.
    D. There are no ships available to take them to America.

Multiple Choice Quiz/ Study Guide Questions *Letters from Rifka*

<u>November 3, 1919, Motziv, Poland through December 1, 1919, Warsaw, Poland</u>
1. One morning, Rifka saves part of her breakfast roll for Saul. Who eats it?
    A. Saul
    B. the family dog
    C. the innkeeper's daughter
    D. a rat

2. Rifka begins to learn _____ when she visits her mother in the hospital in Motziv.
    A. Yiddish
    B. German
    C. Russian
    D. Polish

3. True or False: Two members of Rifka's family die from their typhus illnesses.
    A. True
    B. False

4. Where does Rifka's family go when they leave Motziv?
    A. They go to Oslo, Norway.
    B. They go to Warsaw, Poland.
    C. They go to Moscow, Russia.
    D. They go to London, England.

5. Rifka's older brothers left home and went to America _____ years ago.
    A. two
    B. eight
    C. fourteen
    D. twenty-one

6. What does Rifka do for the peasant girl on the train?
    A. She holds the baby while the girl takes a nap.
    B. She reads to the girl.
    C. She shares her lunch with the girl.
    D. She braids the girl's hair.

7. At the steamship office, Rifka realizes that she got ____ from the peasant girl.
    A. shingles
    B. ringworm
    C. measles
    D. polio

Multiple Choice Quiz/ Study Guide Questions *Letters from Rifka*

November 3, 1919, Motziv, Poland through December 1, 1919, Warsaw, Poland

8. One of the HIAS workers arranges for Rifka to go to _____ and live with a family while she gets treatment at a hospital for the ringworm.
    A. Antwerp, Belgium
    B. Paris, France
    C. Rome, Italy
    D. Berlin, Germany

9. What is Rifka's response to the worker's suggestion?
    A. She says it's a good idea and she will go.
    B. She says she will go but only for one month.
    C. She says she will sneak on the boat and go with her parents.
    D. She says she would rather go back to Berdichev.

10. Rifka agrees to go for treatment, but says she is like _____.
    A. a terminally ill patient
    B. a helpless baby
    C. an orphan
    D. an old woman

Multiple Choice Quiz/ Study Guide Questions *Letters from Rifka*

February 25, 1920, Antwerp, Belgium through September 14, 1920, Antwerp, Belgium
1. Mama gives Rifka the _____ that Papa gave her as a wedding gift. Papa gives her his _____.
      A. diamond ring, Bible
      B. gold locket, prayer shawl
      C. pearl earrings, wedding ring
      D. silver candlesticks, silver cuff links

2. True or False: To celebrate her thirteenth birthday, Rifka has a mitzvah for herself.
      A. True
      B. False

3. What does Rifka learn from Sister Katrina?
      A. She learns to sew her own clothes.
      B. She learns to say her prayers in Latin.
      C. She learns to make the medicine she is using.
      D. She learns to speak Flemish.

4. Sister Katrina tells Rifka she is _____.
      A. brave
      B. thoughtful
      C. clever
      D. funny

5. True or False: Sister Katrina tells Rifka to stay in her room. Sister says Rifka should not go walking around Antwerp alone.
      A. True
      B. False

Multiple Choice Quiz/ Study Guide Questions *Letters from Rifka*

February 25, 1920, Antwerp, Belgium through September 14, 1920, Antwerp, Belgium, continued

6. Rifka wonders if she will ever get a _____.
    A. wig
    B. new dress
    C. letter from Tovah
    D. husband

7. When Rifka gets lost in Antwerp, the person who helps her reminds her of her ___.
    A. father
    B. mother
    C. uncle
    D. cousin

8. Rifka discovers _____ and thinks they are wonderful.
    A. ice cream and chocolate
    B. pizza and soda
    C. movies and popcorn
    D. TV and radio

9. What does Rifka buy for herself?
    A. She buys a notebook and pen.
    B. She buys a book.
    C. She buys lipstick and nail polish.
    D. She buys a hat.

10. Rifka is able to leave for America, but she is concerned because she _____.
    A. gets seasick
    B. is still bald
    C. does not speak English
    D. will miss Sister Katherine

Multiple Choice Quiz/ Study Guide Questions *Letters from Rifka*

September 16, 1920, Somewhere on the Atlantic Ocean
through October 7, 1920, Ellis Island

1. Whom does Rifka meet on the ship?
    A. She meets a girl her age named Anika.
    B. She meets a man who reminds her of her father.
    C. She meets a young sailor named Pieter.
    D. She meets a woman who looks like her aunt.

2. During the storm at sea, the passengers stay in steerage for _____.
    A. one week
    B. four hours
    C. two days
    D. thirty-six hours

3. When Rifka finds out that her friend washed overboard, she _____.
    A. tries to jump overboard herself
    B. feels like she is smothering
    C. faints on the deck
    D. laughs hysterically

4. Rifka ____ until she cannot do it any more.
    A. shouts
    B. throws things
    C. cries
    D. hits the captain

5. Rifka thinks America is a place to _____.
    A. start over
    B. get rich
    C. eat chocolate
    D. buy pretty clothes

6. What does Rifka see as the ship comes into New York Harbor?
    A. She sees the Brooklyn Bridge.
    B. She sees the Empire State Building.
    C. She sees the sunrise over the city.
    D. She sees the Statue of Liberty.

7. True or False: The doctors tell Rifka she will have to get vaccinations for measles and mumps.
    A. True
    B. False

Multiple Choice Quiz/ Study Guide Questions *Letters from Rifka*

<u>September 16, 1920, Somewhere on the Atlantic Ocean
through October 7, 1920, Ellis Island</u>

8. The government thinks Rifka may become a _____.
    A. high-school dropout
    B. juvenile delinquent
    C. social responsibility
    D. missing person

9. True or False: Rifka takes care of a young Russian peasant boy.
    A. True
    B. False

10. Rifka feels good about her actions when she encourages Ilya to _____.
    A. hug her
    B. sleep
    C. pray
    D. eat

Multiple Choice Quiz/ Study Guide Questions *Letters from Rifka*

October 9, 1920, Ellis Island through October 11, 1920, Ellis Island

1. What gift does Saul bring for Rifka?
    A. chocolate
    B. a banana
    C. a book
    D. a doll

2. Saul is surprised that Rifka _____.
    A. knows as much English as she does
    B. has grown three inches and gained weight
    C. is so happy to see him
    D. is so patient about being confined in the hospital

3. Rifka has been bald for _____.
    A. six months
    B. ninety days
    C. one year
    D. four weeks

4. Ilya and Saul struggle over _____.
    A. attention from Rifka
    B. a tin of cookies
    C. Saul's new hat
    D. the Pushkin book

5. Saul says he is glad Rifka is reading the Pushkin book.
    A. True
    B. False

6. As Saul and Rifka are quarreling, she remembers that _____ told her she was a treasure to her family. This calms her down.
    A. Pieter
    B. Tovah
    C. Uncle Avrum
    D. Bubbe Ruth

7. Mama and Papa are working in _____.
    A. a clothing factory
    B. a bakery
    C. a hospital
    D. a subway station

Multiple Choice Quiz/ Study Guide Questions *Letters from Rifka*

October 9, 1920, Ellis Island through October 11, 1920, Ellis Island

8. Rifka tells Saul to buy _____ with the money she saved.
    A. new clothes
    B. a house
    C. food
    D. candlesticks

9. Mama says Rifka is like her ____, who knows how to heal people.
    A. cousin
    B. sister
    C. father
    D. uncle

10. The doctor thinks Ilya is _____.
    A. depressed
    B. a simpleton
    C. violent
    D. dying

Multiple Choice Quiz/ Study Guide Questions *Letters from Rifka*

<u>October 14, 1920, Ellis Island through October 22, 1920, Ellis Island</u>
1. What "trouble" do Ilya and Rifka get into?
  A. They take two extra glasses of milk.
  B. They use a dinner tray to sled in the hallway.
  C. Ilya unrolls a roll of toilet paper.
  D. They throw a ball and break a window.

2. Rifka begins to _____, which comforts her.
  A. play the guitar
  B. study nursing
  C. knit baby blankets
  D. write her own poems

3. True or False: Rifka refuses to put on the kerchief.
  A. True
  B. False

4. True or False: Rifka realizes that she has seen too much of the world to ever go back to Berdichev.
  A. True
  B. False

5. When Ilya's uncle says he loves the boy, Ilya _____.
  A. cries and hugs his uncle
  B. begins reading from the Pushkin book
  C. says, "I love you" in English
  D. dances around the room with Rifka

6. True or False: Ilya has to stay in the hospital for another month.
  A. True
  B. False

7. What action does Ilya take that helps with Mr. Fargate's decision to let Rifka enter the United States?
  A. Ilya asks Mr. Fargate in perfect English.
  B. He says he will not leave without Rifka.
  C. Ilya recites one of Rifka's poems from memory.
  D. He offers to work to pay for her treatment.

Multiple Choice Quiz/ Study Guide Questions *Letters from Rifka*

<u>October 14, 1920, Ellis Island through October 22, 1920, Ellis Island</u>

8. True or False: Rifka discovers that the ringworm has returned.
    A. True
    B. False

9. Saul tells Rifka there are gifts waiting at home. What are they?
    A. There is a prayer shawl for Papa and a toy for the baby.
    B. There are schoolbooks and clothes for Rifka.
    C. There is chocolate and ice cream for everyone.
    D. There are new candlesticks for Mama and paper for Rifka.

10. The family goes back to their home ____.
    A. in Isaac's car
    B. by subway
    C. on the ferry
    D. in a taxi

ANSWER SHEET MULTIPLE CHOICE STUDY GUIDE/QUIZ QUESTIONS
Letters from Rifka

September 2, 1919, Russia through October 5, 1919, Motziv, Poland

1.
2.
3.
4.
5.
6.
7.
8.
9.
10.

November 3, 1919, Motziv, Poland through December 1, 1919, Warsaw, Poland

1.
2.
3.
4.
5.
6.
7.
8.
9.
10.

February 25, 1920, Antwerp, Belgium through September 14, 1920, Antwerp, Belgium

1.
2.
3.
4.
5.
6.
7.
8.
9.
10.

September 16, 1920, Somewhere on the Atlantic Ocean through October 7, 1920, Ellis Island

1.
2.
3.
4.
5.
6.
7.
8.
9.
10.

October 9, 1920, Ellis Island through October 11, 1920, Ellis Island

1.
2.
3.
4.
5.
6.
7.
8.
9.
10.

October 14, 1920, Ellis Island through October 22, 1920, Ellis Island

1.
2.
3.
4.
5.
6.
7.
8.
9.
10.

ANSWER SHEET KEY MULTIPLE CHOICE STUDY GUIDE/QUIZ QUESTIONS
Letters from Rifka

September 2, 1919, Russia through October 5, 1919, Motziv, Poland

1. D
2. A
3. C
4. B
5. A
6. B
7. D
8. C
9. A
10. B

November 3, 1919, Motziv, Poland through December 1, 1919, Warsaw, Poland

1. C
2. D
3. B
4. B
5. C
6. D
7. B
8. A
9. D
10. C

February 25, 1920, Antwerp, Belgium through September 14, 1920, Antwerp, Belgium

1. B
2. A
3. D
4. C
5. B
6. D
7. C
8. A
9. D
10. B

September 16, 1920, Somewhere on the Atlantic Ocean through October 7, 1920, Ellis Island

1. C
2. D
3. B
4. C
5. A
6. D
7. B
8. C
9. A
10. D

October 9, 1920, Ellis Island through October 11, 1920, Ellis Island

1. B
2. A
3. C
4. D
5. B
6. A
7. A
8. D
9. C
10. B

October 14, 1920, Ellis Island through October 22, 1920, Ellis Island

1. C
2. D
3. B
4. A
5. B
6. B
7. C
8. B
9. D
10. A

PREREADING VOCABULARY WORKSHEETS

PREREADING VOCABULARY WORKSHEETS *Letters from Rifka*

September 2, 1919, Russia through October 5, 1919, Motziv, Poland

Part I: Using Prior Knowledge and Contextual Clues
Below are the sentences in which the vocabulary words appear in the text. Read the sentence. Use any clues you can find in the sentence combined with your prior knowledge, and write what you think the italicized word means in the space provided.

1. "You can *distract* the guards, can't you, little sister?" Nathan asked, putting an arm around me.

2. My two giant brothers, Nathan and Saul, *crouched* in separate cars to my left.

3. Behind me, in the dusty corner of a boxcar, sat my own *rucksack*.

4. We *huddled* into your cellar through the black night, planning our escape.

5. Hearing the guards speak this morning, I understood his *precaution*.

6. The guards' bayonets *plunged* into bales and bags and crates in each boxcar.

7. Mama did not seem to notice his *stench*.

8. They returned our clothes to us and our bags, stinking of *fumigation*.

9. The motion of the train *tormented* me.

10. Tovah, my hand is too weak to continue and my eyes *blur* at these tiny letters, but I will write again soon.

Prereading Vocabulary Worksheets *Letters from Rifka*

September 2, 1919, Russia through October 5, 1919, Motziv, Poland

Part II: Determining the Meaning: Match the vocabulary words to their dictionary definitions.

_____ 1. distract   A. gathered together in a tight group

_____ 2. crouched   B. a backpack

_____ 3. rucksack   C. a foul, disgusting smell

_____ 4. huddled   D. become fuzzy or unclear

_____ 5. precaution   E. take attention away from what is happening

_____ 6. plunged   F. pushed firmly into a container

_____ 7. stench   G. inflicted pain or discomfort

_____ 8. fumigation   H. bent close to the ground

_____ 9. tormented   I. action taken to protect against harm

_____ 10. blur   J. a treatment to get rid of bugs or disease

Prereading Vocabulary Worksheets *Letters from Rifka*
November 3, 1919, Motziv, Poland through December 1, 1919, Warsaw, Poland

Part I: Using Prior Knowledge and Contextual Clues
Below are the sentences in which the vocabulary words appear in the text. Read the sentence. Use any clues you can find in the sentence combined with your prior knowledge, and write what you think the italicized word means in the space provided.

1. On my good days, though, I like to look out at the *commotion*.
   _____

2. My stomach knotted painfully, and in spite of my best *intentions* I took another bite of the herring before I closed the closet door.
   _____

3. I was still weak, but I knew I must get up and *stow* the herring and roll in the closet near my cot.
   _____

4. His legs have grown so long since we left Russia. You should see how they *sprout* from his pants.
   _____

5. They are called "cars," and they *prowl* the streets like frenzied wolves.
   _____

6. They are called "cars," and they prowl the streets like *frenzied* wolves
   _____

7. Papa and Mama met with a lady from the HIAS. That is the Hebrew *Immigrant* Aid Society.
   _____

8. The HIAS lady said, "In Antwerp there will be someone from my organization to look out for you, to *monitor* your care.
   _____

9. Tovah, I am like an *orphan* now.
   _____

Prereading Vocabulary Worksheets *Letters from Rifka*

November 3, 1919, Motziv, Poland through December 1, 1919, Warsaw, Poland

Part II: Determining the Meaning: Match the vocabulary words to their dictionary definitions.

_____ 1. commotion   A. a child whose parents are dead

_____ 2. intentions   B. full of uncontrolled anger or excitement

_____ 3. stow   C. plans; purposes

_____ 4. sprout   D. grow quickly

_____ 5. prowl   E. watch over; check on

_____ 6. frenzied   F. someone who settles in a different country

_____ 7. immigrant   G. noisy activity

_____ 8. monitor   H. put something away for future use

_____ 9. orphan   I. move around in a sneaky way

Prereading Vocabulary Worksheets *Letters from Rifka*

February 25, 1920, Antwerp, Belgium through September 14, 1920, Antwerp, Belgium

Part I: Using Prior Knowledge and Contextual Clues
Below are the sentences in which the vocabulary words appear in the text. Read the sentence. Use any clues you can find in the sentence combined with your prior knowledge, and write what you think the italicized word means in the space provided.

1. The night before, Mama had slipped off her gold *locket*. . . . Mama hung the gold chain around my neck.

2. Papa gave me his tallis, his precious prayer *shawl*.

3. It is *odd* to think of Mama and Papa living in such luxury.

4. It is odd to think of Mama and Papa living in such *luxury*.

5. Back in my room, I wove the straws into a Star of David, a *fragile* golden Star of David.

6. Now I write in the *margins* around the poetry.

7. Hannah is like a fairy princess, so *delicate* and beautiful and sweet.

8. She is more practical and *solid* than Hannah.

9. I have found one *advantage* to being on my own. I eat exactly as I please.

10. I am trying to remember your advice, Tovah, to rely on my *wits* and not my looks.

Prereading Vocabulary Worksheets *Letters from Rifka*

February 25, 1920, Antwerp, Belgium through September 14, 1920, Antwerp, Belgium

Part II: Determining the Meaning: Match the vocabulary words to their dictionary definitions.

_____ 1. locket   A. pale, gentle, and soft

_____ 2. shawl   B. a favorable position

_____ 3. odd   C. not strong; easily broken

_____ 4. luxury   D. unusual; strange

_____ 5. fragile   E. a small metal case that holds a picture

_____ 6. margins   F. strong; firm

_____ 7. delicate   G. blank spaces around the print on a page

_____ 8. solid   H. expensive, high quality comfort

_____ 9. advantage   I. a piece of fabric worn over the shoulders

_____ 10. wits   J. intelligence; common sense

Prereading Vocabulary Worksheets *Letters from Rifka*

September 16, 1920, Somewhere on the Atlantic Ocean through October 7, 1920, Ellis Island

Part I: Using Prior Knowledge and Contextual Clues
Below are the sentences in which the vocabulary words appear in the text. Read the sentence. Use any clues you can find in the sentence combined with your prior knowledge, and write what you think the italicized word means in the space provided.

1. Such a *lounge* there is, with a player piano and polished wooden counters.

2. The lounge reminds me of your *salon* back in Berdichev, only much larger.

3. The ocean is so big; everywhere you look in every direction swells this dark, *billowing* water.

4. But when I looked up, Pieter's face was red. "I have work to do," he said, *stammering*.

5. Our ship, which seemed so large and safe when first I boarded, barely survived the *fury* of this storm.

6. The *tempest* started during the night while we slept.

7. I sit in my cabin and wait. Our ship has sent out a *distress* call.

8. I don't know how to tell about what has happened. I feel *numb* and I can't believe.

9. They are holding me, detaining me on Ellis Island, at the hospital for *contagious* diseases.

10. Sometimes it is *convenient* I am small.

Prereading Vocabulary Worksheets *Letters from Rifka*

<u>September 16, 1920, Somewhere on the Atlantic Ocean
through October 7, 1920, Ellis Island</u>

Part II: Determining the Meaning: Match the vocabulary words to their dictionary definitions.

_____ 1. lounge   A. anger

_____ 2. salon   B. useful; helpful

_____ 3. billowing   C. a public room for relaxing

_____ 4. stammering   D. spread from one person to another

_____ 5. fury   E. rolling or flowing upward

_____ 6. tempest   F. not able to feel sensations

_____ 7. distress   G. speaking with many pauses and repetitions

_____ 8. numb   H. an elegant room in a private home

_____ 9. contagious   I. suffering; discomfort

_____ 10. convenient   J. a severe storm with strong winds and rain

Prereading Vocabulary Worksheets *Letters from Rifka*

October 9, 1920, Ellis Island through October 11, 1920, Ellis Island

Part I: Using Prior Knowledge and Contextual Clues
Below are the sentences in which the vocabulary words appear in the text. Read the sentence. Use any clues you can find in the sentence combined with your prior knowledge, and write what you think the italicized word means in the space provided.

1. But Saul came. He *skipped* school and came to see me at the hospital.
   _____

2. I took my brother by the hand and led him into the *ward*.
   _____

3. His eyes twinkled with *mischief*.
   _____

4. Saul looked at me with his head *tilted* to one side.
   _____

5. He lifted his hand to *tousle* my hair, something he used to do when I had blond curls, back in Russia.
   _____

6. Ilya knew how *precious* the little straw star had been to me.
   _____

7. We both *ache* for something we have lost.
   _____

8. I have read to him so often that now he reads *passages* himself.
   _____

9. Any seven-year-old who can read Pushkin is one *clever* boy.
   _____

Prereading Vocabulary Worksheets *Letters from Rifka*

October 9, 1920, Ellis Island through October 11, 1920, Ellis Island

Part II: Determining the Meaning: Match the vocabulary words to their dictionary definitions.

_____ 1. skipped   A. chose to not go to an activity

_____ 2. ward   B. smart; intelligent

_____ 3. mischief   C. a hospital room for several patients

_____ 4. tilted   D. sections of a piece of writing

_____ 5. tousle   E. harmless misbehavior; naughtiness

_____ 6. precious   F. want something a lot

_____ 7. ache   G. slanted; leaning at an angle

_____ 8. passages   H. much loved and valued

_____ 9. clever   I. tangle or mess up hair

Prereading Vocabulary Worksheets *Letters from Rifka*

October 14, 1920, Ellis Island through October 22, 1920, Ellis Island

Part I: Using Prior Knowledge and Contextual Clues
Below are the sentences in which the vocabulary words appear in the text. Read the sentence. Use any clues you can find in the sentence combined with your prior knowledge, and write what you think the italicized word means in the space provided.

1. I grabbed his arm, holding it away, while *frantically* I started rolling the paper back.
   _____

2. "Ilya unrolled toilet paper," I said, believing Ilya had *committed* one of the worst offenses he could ever commit here.
   _____

3. "Ilya unrolled toilet paper," I said, believing Ilya had committed one of the worst *offenses* he could ever commit here.
   _____

4. Yet even in my fear I cannot *deny* the beauty of this place.
   _____

5. Mr. Fargate said, "This boy shows *minimal* intelligence."
   _____

6. Ilya was being as *stubborn* as ever.
   _____

7. Mr. Fargate lifted the stamp, the *deportation* stamp.
   _____

8. Ilya pulled it back, *clasping* the book to his chest.
   _____

9. "Not very *modest*, is she?"
   _____

10. *Compassion* is a part of medicine you can't teach, Mr. Fargate.
    _____

Prereading Vocabulary Worksheets *Letters from Rifka*

October 14, 1920, Ellis Island through October 22, 1920, Ellis Island

Part II: Determining the Meaning: Match the vocabulary words to their dictionary definitions.

_____ 1. frantically   A. disagree; say something is not true

_____ 2. committed   B. a very small amount

_____ 3. offenses   C. kindness; consideration

_____ 4. deny   D. quickly and with excitement

_____ 5. minimal   E. humble; not showing off

_____ 6. stubborn   F. wrongdoings against usual standards

_____ 7. deportation   G. holding tightly

_____ 8. clasping   H. willful; not cooperative

_____ 9. modest   I. removal of a foreigner from a country

_____ 10. compassion   J. done something wrong

ANSWER SHEET PREREADING VOCABULARY WORKSHEETS
Letters from Rifka

September 2, 1919, Russia through October 5, 1919, Motziv, Poland	November 3, 1919, Motziv, Poland through December 1, 1919, Warsaw, Poland	February 25, 1920, Antwerp, Belgium through September 14, 1920, Antwerp, Belgium
1. E	1. G	1. E
2. H	2. C	2. I
3. B	3. H	3. D
4. A	4. D	4. H
5. I	5. I	5. C
6. F	6. B	6. G
7. C	7. F	7. A
8. J	8. E	8. F
9. G	9. A	9. B
10. D		10. J

September 16, 1920, Somewhere on the Atlantic Ocean through October 7, 1920, Ellis Island	October 9, 1920, Ellis Island through October 11, 1920, Ellis Island	October 14, 1920, Ellis Island through October 22, 1920, Ellis Island
1. C	1. A	1. D
2. H	2. C	2. J
3. E	3. E	3. F
4. G	4. G	4. A
5. A	5. I	5. B
6. J	6. H	6. H
7. I	7. F	7. I
8. F	8. D	8. G
9. D	9. B	9. E
10. B		10. C

DAILY LESSON PLANS

Daily Lesson Plans *Letters from Rifka*

LESSON ONE

Objectives
1. To introduce the *Letters from Rifka* unit
2. To distribute books, study guides and other related materials
3. To give students background information about *Letters from Rifka*

Activity #1

A&E Home Video has a Multimedia Classroom American History Series which has one volume on Ellis Island. The DVD has an accompanying Interactive Lesson Plan CD-ROM with transcripts of the DVD segments, related questions for each segment, and activity ideas for each segment. If you choose to acquire and show the DVD as background information, you will need more than one class period. The whole DVD takes a couple of hours to see, and if you decide to use any of the materials that accompany the DVD, it will take even longer. It is, however, in this editor's opinion, well worth the time and money spent because the DVD is right on point with many of the events, comments, and issues presented in *Letters from Rifka*. To purchase the Ellis Island video, go to www.history.com click on STORE and type in Ellis Island in the search field.

Activity #2

Distribute books, study guides, and reading assignments. Explain in detail how students are to use these materials.

Study Guides Students should read the study guide questions for each reading assignment prior to beginning the reading assignment to get a feeling for what events and ideas are important in the section they are about to read. After reading the section, students will (as a class or individually) answer the questions to review the important events and ideas from that section of the book. Students should keep the study guides as study materials for the unit test.

Vocabulary Prior to each a reading assignment, students will do vocabulary work related to the section of the book they are about to read. Following the completion of the reading of the book, there will be a vocabulary review of all the words used in the vocabulary assignments. Students should keep their vocabulary work as study materials for the unit test.

Reading Assignment Sheet You need to fill in the reading assignment sheet to let students know by when their reading has to be completed. You can either write the assignment sheet up on a side blackboard or bulletin board and leave it there for students to see each day, or you can "ditto" copies for each student to have. In either case, you should advise students to become very familiar with the reading assignments so they know what is expected of them.

Daily Lesson Plans *Letters from Rifka*
LESSON ONE, continued

<u>Extra Activities Center</u> The Unit Resource Materials portion of this LitPlan contains suggestions for an extra library of related books and articles in your classroom as well as crossword and word search puzzles. Make an extra activities center in your room where you will keep these materials for students to use. (Bring the books and articles in from the library and keep several copies of the puzzles on hand.) Explain to students that these materials are available for students to use when they finish reading assignments or other class work early.

<u>Nonfiction Assignment Sheet</u> Explain to students that they each are to read at least one non-fiction piece from the in-class library at some time during the unit. Students will fill out a nonfiction assignment sheet after completing the reading to help you (the teacher) evaluate their reading experiences and to help the students think about and evaluate their own reading experiences.

<u>Books</u> Each school has its own rules and regulations regarding student use of school books. Advise students of the procedures that are normal for your school.

<u>Notebook or Unit Folder</u> You may want the students to keep all of their worksheets, notes, and other papers for the unit together in a binder or notebook. During the first class meeting, tell them how you want them to arrange the folder. Make divider pages for vocabulary worksheets, Prereading study guide questions, review activities, notes, and tests. You may want to give a grade for accuracy in keeping the folder.

<u>Activity #3</u>
Explain that Aleksandr Pushkin was a Russian writer who lived from 1799-1873. His first poem was published when he was 14. Some consider him to be Russia's most famous poet. Have students follow along as you read a few of the Pushkin quotes aloud to them. Discuss their meaning. You may want to discuss all of the quotes at once, or discuss each quote in the context of the chapters as students read.

THE PUSHKIN QUOTES
Letters From Rifka

. . . and from
The gloomy land of lonely exile
To a new country bade me come . . . .

. . . And with a sword he clove my breast,
Plucked out the heart he made beat higher,
And in my stricken bosom pressed
Instead a coal of living fire . . . .

Casual gift, oh, gift unutile,
Life, why wert thou given me?
Why should Fate thus grant us futile
Terms of doomed mortality? . . .

A thirst in spirit, through the gloom
Of an unpeopled waste I blundered . . .

. . . In hope, in torment, we are turning
Toward freedom, waiting her command . . .

. . . Goal, there can be none before me,
Empty-hearted, idle-willed.
Life's monotony rolls o'er me,
Tired with longings unfulfilled.

. . . As conquered by the last cold air,
When winter whistles in the wind,
Alone upon a branch that's bare
A trembling leaf is left behind.

. . . Sleep evades me, there's no light:
Darkness wraps the earth with slumber,
Only weary tickings number
The slow hours of the night. . . .

With freedom's seed the desert sowing,
I walked before the morning star . . .

. . . And I shall know some savor of elation
Amidst the cares, the woes, and the vexation . . .

The Pushkin Quotes 2
Letters From Rifka

. . . The sister of misfortune, Hope,
In the under-darkness dumb
Speaks joyful courage to your heart:
The day desired will come . . . .

We numbered many in the ship,
Some spread the sails, some pulled, together,
The mighty oars; 'twas placid weather.
The rudder in his steady grip,
Our helmsman silently was steering
The heavy galley through the sea,
While I, from doubts and sorrows free,
Sang to the crew . . .

. . . When suddenly,
A storm! And the wide sea was rearing . . .
The helmsman and the crew were lost.
No sailor by the storm was tossed
Ashore–but I, who had been singing.
I chant the songs I loved of yore,
And on the sunned and rocky shore
I dry my robes, all wet and clinging.

. . . And thoughts stir bravely in my head, and rhymes
Run forth to meet them on light feet, and fingers
Reach for the pen. . .

. . . Give me your hand. I will return
At the beginning of October . . .

. . . My path is bleak–before me stretch my morrows:
A tossing sea, foreboding toil and sorrows.
And yet I don not wish to die, be sure;
I want to live–think, suffer, and endure . . .

. . . I am lean and shaven, but alive;
. . . And there is hope that I may thrive . . . .

. . . They say ill things of the last days of Autumn:
But I, friend reader, not a one will hear;
Her quiet beauty touches me as surely
As does a wistful child, to no one dear . . . .

The Pushkin Quotes 3
Letters From Rifka

. . . Oh, mournful season that delights the eyes,
Your farewell beauty captivates my spirit.
I love the pomp of Nature's fading dyes,
The forests, garmented in gold and purple,
The rush of noisy wind, and the pale skies
Half-hidden by the clouds in darkling billows,
And the rare sun-ray and the early frost,
And threats of grizzled Winter, heard and lost . . .

. . . This heart its leave of you has taken;
Accept, my distant dear, love's close,
As does the wife death leaves forsaken,
As does the exile's comrade, shaken
And mute, who clasps him once, and goes.

. . . The heavy-hanging chains will fall,
The walls will crumble at a word;
And Freedom greet you in the light,
And brothers give you back the sword.

Storm-clouds dim the sky; the tempest
Weaves the snow in patterns wild . . .

. . . Like a beast the gale is howling,
And now wailing like a child . . .

. . . I like the grapes whose clusters ripen
Upon the hillside in the sun . . .

I leave to you the low and leaning room,
where once we drank the honey-sweetened tea,
and bowed our heads in prayer and waited there,
for cossacks with their boots and bayonets,

I leave behind my cousins, young and dear;
They'll never know the freedom I have known,
Or learn as I have learned, that kindness dwells,
In hearts that have no fear.

Daily Lesson Plans *Letters from Rifka*

LESSON TWO

Objectives
1. To do the prereading work for the chapters titled "September 2, 1919, Russia" through "October 5, 1919, Motziv, Poland"
2. To read the chapters titled "September 2, 1919, Russia through "October 5, 1919, Motziv, Poland"
3. To become acquainted with the Nonfiction Assignment

Activity #1

Show students how to preview the study questions and do the vocabulary work for the chapters titled "September 2, 1919, Russia" through "October 5, 1919, Motziv, Poland." Encourage students to take notes as they read. If students own their books, encourage them to use highlighters or colored pens to mark important passages and the answers to the study guide questions.

Activity #2

Read the first few pages aloud to students to set the mood for the novel. Then have students read the remaining pages in the assignment orally. Either call on students or ask for volunteers, whichever works best with your class. Be sure to give students who need practice reading orally the opportunity to do so, even if it slows down the reading schedule a little. If you have not given students a grade for oral reading this quarter, during the reading of this novel would be a good time to grade them. Be sure to let them know that they will be evaluated and tell them the criteria you will use.

If students do not complete reading this assignment in class, they should finish it on their own time prior to the next class period.

Activity #3

Distribute copies of the Nonfiction Assignment Sheet and go over it in detail with the students. Explain to students that they each are to read at least one nonfiction piece at some time during the unit. This could be a book, a magazine article, or information from an encyclopedia or the Internet. Students will fill out a Nonfiction Assignment Sheet after completing the reading to help you (the teacher) evaluate their reading experiences and to help the students think about and evaluate their own reading. Encourage students to read about topics that are related to the theme of the novel.

NONFICTION ASSIGNMENT SHEET
Letters from Rifka
(To be completed after reading the required nonfiction article.)

Name _____ Date _____ Class _____

Title of Nonfiction Read _____

Written by _____ Publication Date _____

Web Site Address (if applicable) _____

I. Factual Summary: Write a summary of the piece you read.

II. Vocabulary:
    1. Which vocabulary words were difficult?

    2. What did you do to help yourself understand the words?

III. Interpretation: What was the main point the author wanted you to get from reading his/her work?

IV. Criticism:
    1. Which points of the piece did you agree with or find easy to believe? Why?

    2. With which points of the piece did you disagree or find difficult to believe? Why?

V. Personal Response:
    1. What did you think about this piece?

    2. How does this piece help you understand the novel *Letters from Rifka*?

Daily Lesson Plans *Letters from Rifka*

LESSON THREE

Objectives
1. To review the main ideas and events from the chapters titled "September 2, 1919, Russia" through "October 5, 1919, Motziv, Poland"
2. To do the prereading work for the chapters titled "November 3, 1919, Motziv, Poland" through "December 1, 1919, Warsaw, Poland"
3. To read the chapters titled "November 3, 1919, Motziv, Poland" through "December 1, 1919, Warsaw, Poland"

Activity #1

Give students time to answer the study guide questions from the chapters titled "September 2, 1919, Russia" through "October 5, 1919, Motziv, Poland" and then discuss the answers in detail. Write the answers on the board or overhead projector film so students can have the correct answers for study purposes.

Note: It is a good practice in public speaking and leadership skills for individual students to take charge of leading the discussion of the study questions. Perhaps a different student could go to the front of the class and lead the discussion each day that the study questions are discussed during the unit.

Activity #2

Give students about ten or fifteen minutes to complete the Prereading vocabulary worksheet and preview the study guide questions for the chapters titled "November 3, 1919, Motziv, Poland" through "December 1, 1919, Warsaw, Poland"

Activity #3

Have students work with partners to read the chapters. Tell them to take turns reading aloud. Suggest that they stop after each two pages to orally summarize what they have read, and to answer the pertinent study questions.

Daily Lesson Plans *Letters from Rifka*

LESSON FOUR

Objectives
1. To review the main events and ideas in the chapters titled "November 3, 1919, Motziv, Poland" through "December 1, 1919, Warsaw, Poland"
2. To begin to identify examples of character traits

Activity #1

Have partners answer the study guide questions and review their prereading vocabulary worksheets. Go over the answers with the class. Then have partners write a few additional questions about the chapters. Have each pair read their questions aloud to the class and call on other students to answer.

Activity #2

Explain that in a novel such as *Letters from Rifka*, the author acquaints the reader with the characters by describing character traits such as physical attributes, thoughts, and feelings. Words to describe character traits include strong, weak, polite, rude, selfish, selfless, clever, kind, prejudiced, and open-minded. The author develops these traits by describing what the characters do, say, and think. Usually the main character is most fully developed, while minor characters may have only a few traits developed, or partly developed. Remind students that in this historical fiction novel, Karen Hesse is developing characters loosely based on some of her family members. She wants the characters to seem real, so she portrays them as realistically as possible. She gives more details about Rifka, since she is the central character. However, the reader can still learn something about the rest of the characters through the author's descriptions.

Have students look for the character traits of Rifka and one other character of their choice as they read. You may want to have students write the name of their second choice character on a sign-up sheet so that all other characters in the book are covered. Distribute copies of the Character Traits Chart (included). Ask students to fill in what they have learned about Rifka and the other character so far. Tell them they should continue to be aware of the character traits of both characters as they read, and that they will continue the discussion and complete more of the chart during Lesson Seventeen. As an extension, students can copy the character traits chart and use it to record information about additional characters in the book.

CHARACTER TRAITS CHART
Letters from Rifka

Directions: Fill in the charts for Rifka and one other character with examples from the novel.

Rifka's Character Traits	Words, Thoughts, or Actions That Illustrate the Trait
1.	
2.	
3.	

_____'s Character Traits	Words, Thoughts, or Actions That Illustrate the Trait
	1.
	2.
	3.

Daily Lesson Plans *Letters from Rifka*

LESSON FIVE

Objectives
1. To give students the opportunity to practice reading orally
2. To give the teacher the opportunity to evaluate students' reading skills

Activity #1
Tell students their oral reading ability will be evaluated. Show them copies of the Oral Reading Evaluation form and discuss it. Model correct intonation and expression by reading the first few paragraphs of the chapter titled "November 3, 1919, Motziv, Poland" aloud.

Activity #2
Give students time to look through the chapters they have read so far to find a few paragraphs they would like to read aloud. Allow time for students to practice. You may want to allow partners or small groups to read aloud together. They could take the roles of the characters and also assign a narrator.

Activity #3
Call on individuals, partners, or groups to read their paragraphs aloud. Encourage the other students to follow along in their books. If you have a student who is unwilling or unable to read aloud in front of the group, make arrangements to do his or her evaluation privately at another time. Mark the oral reading evaluation forms as the students read.

Activity #4
After students have read aloud, ask them to evaluate their own performance. Discuss with the class the things they do well as oral readers, and how they could all improve. Suggest that students spend a few minutes reading aloud to someone at home in the evening.

ORAL READING EVALUATION
Letters from Rifka

Name _____ Class _____ Date _____

SKILL	EXCELLENT	GOOD	AVERAGE	FAIR	POOR
FLUENCY	5	4	3	2	1
CLARITY	5	4	3	2	1
AUDIBILITY	5	4	3	2	1
PRONUNCIATION	5	4	3	2	1
_____	5	4	3	2	1
_____	5	4	3	2	1
TOTAL GRADE	5	4	3	2	1

COMMENTS:

Daily Lesson Plans *Letters from Rifka*

LESSON SIX

Objectives
1. To personally involve students with the issue of immigration
2. To help students appreciate the good things America offers its people
3. To show students that not every country is like the United States
4. To give students the opportunity to express their personal opinions
5. To evaluate students' writing

NOTES:
Prior to this lesson, find three people in your school or community who have immigrated to the United States and are willing to share their stories with your class. If possible, choose people from three different countries. You may need to make arrangements for translation if your immigrants do not yet speak English well.

Activity #1
Introduce your speakers and their relevance to *Rifka*. You might say something like, "The book we have been reading, *Letters From Rifka*, is about a family of Jewish Russians who immigrated to the United States during World War I to avoid persecution in Russia. People from many countries all over the world have immigrated to the United States throughout our history–and continue to do so today. We are glad to have with us several immigrants who have graciously agreed to share their stories with you today. (Introduce your guests)

Give each of your guests time to tell their stories–who they are, where they came from, why they came to America, how they got here, who else came with them (if anyone), what life was like where they came from and how life is here for them, etc. If your guests are willing, give students a little time to ask a few questions, if they have any.

Be sure to appropriately thank your guests. You might consider having students write thank you notes or letters to them.

Activity #2
Distribute Writing Assignment #1 and discuss the directions in detail. Allow students the remainder of the class period to work on this assignment. Give students additional in class time to complete the assignment if necessary; otherwise, let them know when the assignment is due and collect it on that date.

Activity #3
Distribute copies of the Writing Evaluation Form (included in this Lit Plan.) Explain to students that during Lesson Nine you will be holding individual writing conferences about this writing assignment. Make sure they are familiar with the criteria on the Writing Evaluation Form.

WRITING ASSIGNMENT #1 *Letters from Rifka*
Writing to Express a Personal Opinion

PROMPT

Have students reread the chapter that is titled "November 27, 1919 en route to Warsaw." Point out the quote by the Polish peasant girl who talked with Rifka: *She said, "Why would you want to go to America? You can do everything you want right here. I would never leave Poland."* Rifka did not respond to the girl's question. Imagine that you are an immigrant coming to America. How would you answer the question?

PREWRITING

Remember that a personal opinion piece should include your thoughts and feelings. As often as possible, support these thoughts and feelings with factual evidence or examples. Make a list of reasons that Rifka or another immigrant might have for leaving their home country and coming to America. Organize the list starting with the most important or most convincing reasons first, and proceeding to the least important reason. You may want to make a concept web with the word *America* in the center. List positive words to describe America. You may also want to do some research on one or more foreign countries so that you have facts to use to compare that country with America.

DRAFTING

You will probably want to use the first person point of view. Refer to the concept web you developed as you write. Write your first draft. Check to make sure you are including your opinion. Use as many descriptive words and images as you can. You may want to use a thesaurus to help you get a variety of words and their exact meanings.

PEER CONFERENCING/REVISING

When you finish the rough draft of your personal opinion piece, ask another student to read it. After reading your rough draft, the student should tell you what he/she liked best about your work, which parts were difficult to understand, and ways in which your work could be improved. Reread your text considering your critic's comments, and make the revisions you think are necessary.

PROOFREADING/EDITING

Do a final proofreading of your opinion piece, double checking your grammar, spelling, organization, and the clarity of your ideas. Turn the piece into your teacher for grading. Follow your teacher's guidelines for completing the final draft of your piece.

FINAL DRAFT

Follow your teacher's directions for making a final copy of your paper.

WRITING EVALUATION FORM
Letters from Rifka

Name _____ Date _____

Writing Assignment # _____

Circle One for Each Item:

Composition	Excellent	Good	Fair	Poor
Style	Excellent	Good	Fair	Poor
Grammar	Excellent	Good	Fair	Poor
Spelling	Excellent	Good	Fair	Poor
Punctuation	Excellent	Good	Fair	Poor
Legibility	Excellent	Good	Fair	Poor

Strengths:

Weaknesses:

Comments/Suggestions:

Daily Lesson Plans *Letters from Rifka*

LESSON SEVEN

Objectives
    1. To do the prereading work for the chapters titled "February 25, 1920, Antwerp, Belgium" through "September 14, 1920, Antwerp, Belgium"
    2. To reads chapters titled "February 25, 1920, Antwerp, Belgium" through "September 14, 1920, Antwerp, Belgium"
    3. To review the main ideas and events from the chapters titled "February 25, 1920, Antwerp, Belgium" through "September 14, 1920, Antwerp, Belgium"
    4. To identify and discuss elements of the setting in the book

Activity #1
    Have students complete the prereading work for the chapters individually and then check their answers in small groups.

Activity #2
    Have students read chapters titled "February 25, 1920, Antwerp, Belgium" through "September 14, 1920, Antwerp, Belgium". This can be done as a class or individual.

Activity #3
    Review the main ideas and events in chapters titled "February 25, 1920, Antwerp, Belgium" through "September 14, 1920, Antwerp, Belgium".

Activity #4
    Explain to students that the setting includes the time and place of a story. Knowing the time and place will help them understand the story because they will understand why characters do certain things, why events happen, and why problems occur. The setting helps the readers get a visual image of a place and a time. Remind students that all or part of the setting may change during the course of a story. For example, characters may travel to another place, or a story may take place over an extended period of time. Both of these elements are present in *Letters from Rifka.*
    Tell students that the setting is more important in some stories than in others. The setting is very important in *Letters from Rifka.* That is evident since the names of places, as well as specific dates, are used as chapter titles. The setting can support the author's purpose for writing the story.
    Work with students to begin filling out the Setting Graphic Organizer (included.) Have students go through the chapters they have already read and look for evidence of the setting.
    Tell students to continue taking notes on the organizer as they read. They will review the completed organizer in Lesson Fifteen. At this time, discuss with students how the setting supports the author's purpose for writing the story.

SETTING GRAPHIC ORGANIZER

Directions: Fill in details about the setting of *Letters from Rifka*

Chapter	Details About the Time	Details About the Place

Draw your impression of one of the settings.

Daily Lesson Plans *Letters from Rifka*

LESSON EIGHT

Objectives
1. To do the prereading work for the chapters titled "September 16, 1920, Somewhere on the Atlantic Ocean" through "October 7, 1920, Ellis Island"
2. To read the chapters titled "September 16, 1920, Somewhere on the Atlantic Ocean" through "October 7, 1920, Ellis Island"
3. To review the main ideas and events from the chapters titled "September 16, 1920, Somewhere on the Atlantic Ocean" through "October 7, 1920, Ellis Island"
4. To catch up on any unfinished work
5. To study for the upcoming quiz

Activity # 1
Give students about fifteen minutes to do the prereading and vocabulary work for the chapters titled "September 16, 1920, Somewhere on the Atlantic Ocean" through "October 7, 1920, Ellis Island."

Activity #2
Give students most of the remainder of the period to silently read the chapters titled "September 16, 1920, Somewhere on the Atlantic Ocean" through "October 7, 1920, Ellis Island."

Activity #3
Allow about fifteen minutes at the end of the class period to go over the study questions together. Tell students they will have a quiz on the chapters titled "September 2, 1919, Russia" through "October 7, 1920, Ellis Island" during the next class period. Give students time to go through their study guides and notes to see if they are missing any information. Provide assistance as necessary.

Activity #4
Give students any remaining class time to study for the quiz.

Daily Lesson Plans *Letters from Rifka*

LESSON NINE

Objectives
1. To demonstrate understanding of the main ideas and events in the chapters titled "September 2, 1919, Russia" through "October 7, 1920, Ellis Island"
2. To evaluate students' writing via individual writing conferences
3. To revise Writing Assignment #1 based on the teacher's suggestions
4. To review and study the chapter and vocabulary work covered so far

Activity #1

Quiz-Distribute quizzes (multiple choice study questions for the chapters titled "September 2, 1919, Russia" through "October 7, 1920, Ellis Island" and give students about twenty minutes to complete them. Correct and grade the papers as a class. You may want to have students exchange papers or allow them to correct their own work. As an extra credit assignment, have students find the correct answers to any questions they missed and rewrite any "false" answers to be true. Collect the quizzes for recording the grades.

Activity #2

Call students individually to your desk or some other private area of the classroom. Discuss their papers from Writing Assignment #1. Use the completed Writing Evaluation form as a basis for your critique.

Activity #3

Students should use the class time when they are not in conference with you to do any of the following: work on their nonfiction reading assignment; revise Writing Assignment #1; work on the Character Traits and Setting Charts; review the study guide questions and answers and prereading vocabulary worksheets they have completed so far.

Daily Lesson Plans *Letters from Rifka*

LESSON TEN

<u>Objectives</u>
1. To do the prereading work for the chapters titled "October 9, 1920, Ellis Island through October 11, 1920, Ellis Island"
2. To read the chapters titled "October 9, 1920, Ellis Island through October 11, 1920, Ellis Island"

<u>Activity #1</u>
Give students ten or fifteen minutes to complete the prereading work for the chapters. Take time to check the vocabulary matching section so students have the correct answers.

<u>Activity #2:</u>
Have students read the chapters independently. If they finish reading and still have class time left, they can start answering the study guide questions or work on one of their charts. Tell them the study guide questions will be due at the next class period.

Daily Lesson Plans *Letters from Rifka*

LESSON ELEVEN

Objectives
    1. To demonstrate understanding of the main ideas and events in the chapters titled "October 9, 1920, Ellis Island through October 11, 1920, Ellis Island"
    2. To identify the sequence of events in the novel

Activity #1
    Have students write the letters A, B, C, D on strips of paper. Write the multiple choice questions for the chapters titled "October 9, 1920, Ellis Island through October 11, 1920, Ellis Island" on chart paper, or make a transparency of the pages and show them on the overhead projector. Ask volunteers to read aloud the questions and answer choices. Tell students to hold up the paper strip that has the letter for their answer choice.

Activity #2
    Ask students to tell what they know about sequence in a novel and why it is important. Write their responses on the board and add any more information that they need to know. Ask students how the sequence is shown in *Letters from Rifka* (in the chapter titles). Discuss the effectiveness of showing the sequence in this way. Using a long roll of shelf paper or something similar, have students create a timeline for the main dates and events in *Letters from Rifka*. Show students how to calculate the amount of time that elapsed from Rifka's first journal entry to the last, and then how to space the markings on the timeline so that they are accurate. Encourage students to add magazine pictures and/or their own illustrations to the timeline. Then ask questions and have students use the timeline to answer them. For example: *Did Rifka lose her hair before or after the family left Berdichev?* Invite students to form their own questions.

Daily Lesson Plans *Letters from Rifka*

LESSON TWELVE

Objectives
1. To become acquainted with Writing Assignment #2
2. To complete Writing Assignment #2

Activity #1

Distribute Writing Assignment #2. Discuss the directions in detail and give students the rest of the class period to complete the assignment. You may want the students to work with partners or in small groups.

LESSON THIRTEEN

Objectives
1. To preview the study questions and vocabulary for the chapters titled "October 14, 1920, Ellis Island" through "October 22, 1920, Ellis Island."
2. To read the chapters titled "October 14, 1920, Ellis Island" through "October 22, 1920, Ellis Island."
3. To review the main ideas and events from the chapters titled "October 14, 1920, Ellis Island" through "October 22, 1920, Ellis Island."

Activity #1

Divide the class into small groups. Have the groups work together to do the prereading and vocabulary work. Group members can decide how they want to approach the work. Suggest that they may want to assign a few vocabulary words to each member, and have each member teach those vocabulary words to the rest of the group. Or, they may have each member work independently, then gather as a group to go over the vocabulary words.

Activity #2

Tell the students to stay in the same groups as they formed to complete Activity #1. Have them sit in a small circle and take turns reading aloud quietly. As they come to the answer to one of the study questions, they should stop, discuss the question and answer, and write their response.

Activity #3

Have students continue to sit with the same group. Tell each group to choose a spokesperson. Discuss the answers to the study guide questions with the class, having each spokesperson respond for their group.

WRITING ASSIGNMENT #2 *Letters from Rifka*
Writing to Inform

PROMPT
Rifka had many adventures and experiences from the time she left Berdichev until she arrived in New York City. Now she is ready to help other young immigrants benefit from her experiences. Your writing assignment is to take the point of view of Rifka and write a set of travel tips for immigrants.

PREWRITING
Make a list of the things that Rifka did, such as learn local languages and sample new foods. You may also want to add travel tips that you have used, or that you have read about. Organize your list from most to least important.

DRAFTING
Decide on a format for your travel tips. You may want to make a poster or a brochure, or design a web site. Use strong action verbs for your tips. Think of clever ways to give the information. Make your own illustrations or use pictures from other sources.

PEER CONFERENCING/REVISING
When you finish the rough draft of your information piece, ask another student to read it. After reading your rough draft, the student should tell you what he/she liked best about your work, which parts were difficult to understand, and ways in which your work could be improved. Your reader should also be able to summarize your travel tips based on your text. Reread your text considering your critic's comments, and make the revisions you think are necessary.

PROOFREADING/EDITING
Do a final proofreading of your information piece, double checking your grammar, spelling, organization, and the clarity of your ideas. Turn the piece into your teacher for grading.

FINAL DRAFT
Follow your teacher's directions for making a final copy of your paper.

Daily Lesson Plans *Letters from Rifka*

LESSON FOURTEEN

Objective
To discuss *Letters from Rifka* at the interpretive and critical levels

Activity # 1
Use the Extra Writing Assignments/Discussions Questions as a springboard for discussing the novel in more depth. Either write answers to the questions on the board or simply have students take notes during the discussion.
NOTE: This is a good time to combine activities to have students practice note-taking skills. If time permits (or if you can make time), allow students to just take notes during the discussion. You should take notes answering the questions on an overhead projector transparency during the discussion, as if you were answering the questions on the board for students to copy. Leave the projector off during the discussion. When the discussion is complete, go back, turn on the projector and briefly review the ideas students should have written into their notes. Allow time for students to fix their notes so they have all the information you want them to have.
If there is extra time, encourage students to ask additional questions.

LESSON FIFTEEN

Objectives
    1. To discuss selected quotations from the book
    2. To discuss the completed graphic organizers

Activity # 1
Read the quotations with students. First ask them to give details from memory about the scene in the book from which the quote came. Then have students check in the book to verify the details. Discuss the importance of the quote.
Challenge students to memorize one or more of the quotations and recite it for the class.

NOTE: Instead of doing all of the quotes, you might choose specific ones based on your class's level. If so, you may need to edit the unit test(s) accordingly.

Activity # 2
Go over the completed Character Traits Chart and Setting Chart with students. Allow time for students to ask questions and make any necessary corrections. Remind students to keep these charts and use them as study aids when they prepare for their test.
You may want to post correctly completed copies of the charts on a bulletin board and/or the class Web site for future reference.

EXTRA WRITING ASSIGNMENTS / DISCUSSION QUESTIONS
Letters from Rifka

Interpretive
1. Explain the significance of the title of the novel.
2. Explain the significance of each chapter title of the novel.
3. Plot Rifka's growth as a character throughout the novel.
4. What are the main conflicts in the novel? How are they resolved?
5. How important is the setting to the story?
6. Discuss the changes in Rifka over the course of the novel.
7. How important is the sequence to the story?

Critical
8. What is the point of view of the novel? How does it affect your understanding of the story? How would the story be different if it were written from the point of view of another character or from a third person omniscient narrator?
9. Is the story of *Rifka* believable? Explain why or why not.
10. Does the voice of the main character sound like the voice of a twelve/thirteen-year-old girl? Explain why it does or does not.
11. Are the characters in *Letters from Rifka* stereotypes? If so, explain which ones are stereotypes and the usefulness of employing stereotypes in *Letters from Rifka*. If they are not, explain how they merit individuality.
12. Discuss the imagery used in the book. How vivid is it? How effective is it?
13. Describe Karen Hesse's writing style. Explain why you do or do not like it.

Personal Response
14. Imitate Karen Hesse's writing style as you write a story about something which has recently happened to you or an event which has recently taken place at school.
15. Choose one scene from *Letters from Rifka* and write it as a play. Then, explain the difficulties, if any, you encountered in doing so.
16. Did you enjoy reading *Letters from Rifka?* Explain why or why not.
17. *Letters from Rifka* has several difficult or tragic events. Which was the most serious or moving, and why?
18. Which of the characters did you like and why? Was there a character you disliked? Why?
19. Which scene or event in the book did you like most? Why?
20. The author incorporated a real situation, persecuted Russian Jews leaving their home in Russian and immigrating to America, into a fictional story. How effective was this device? Did it add to or take away from your enjoyment of the story?
21. Did Rifka's experiences change the way you look at yourself? How?
22. Did Ilya's experiences change the way you look at yourself? How?
23. Would you recommend this book to another student? Why or why not?
24. If you could change one thing about the book, what would it be? Why?
25. Have you read any other stories similar to *Letters from Rifka*? If so, tell about them.
26. What questions would you like to ask the author?
27. What else would you like to know about Rifka and her family?
28. Did you like reading the quotes from Pushkin? Why or why not?

QUOTATIONS
Letters from Rifka

Discuss the significance of the following quotations from *Letters from Rifka*:

1. "You can distract the guards, can't you, little sister?"

2. "I've come to warn Saul. The soldiers will soon follow. They will take him into the army."

3. "Nathan isn't going to return. Hurry! We must pack!"

4. "I'm here to take the train. My mother has found me work in a wealthy house."

5. Shalom, my little house. Shalom, my family; shalom, Berdichev, and my dear little grandmother, Bubbe Ruth. Shalom, Hannah and Aunt Anna and Uncle Avrum, but most of all, Tovah, Shalom to you.

6. I thought of the things the Russians had taken from my family as I stood in the train yard and I was angry. Why, Tovah? Why is it that if a Russian peasant does not get what he wants, he feels justified in stealing it from a Jew?

7. "So they stole our candlesticks," Mama said. "It could be worse, Rifka, much worse. Stop sniffling and finish getting dressed."

8. "You must say nothing about the nature of her illness to anyone," the medical student told Papa. "Not even to your cousin. As for the child, she will probably die. Most do. That's how it goes with typhus."

9. "Thief!" I cried in Russian. "Give me back my food!"

10. Saul said, "Next time, don't save your food, Rifka. Eat it. Then she can't take it from you."

11. "I used to fix my cousin's hair," I said in Polish. "I could fix yours so you will look nice for your sister. . . if you like."

12. She said, "Why would you want to go to America? You can do everything you want right here. I would never leave Poland."

13. "No," the doctor said. "I am sorry. Your daughter cannot join you. Our company will not sell her passage to America."

14. "There you are! Thief! You steal my oranges! Help! Police! What monster are you, that you steal from an old man!"/ "I did not! I cried. "I paid you. You took all the money I had!"

15. I said, "If I can't go to America, please send me back to Berdichev."

Quotations *Letters from Rifka*

16. "Tovah, I am like an orphan now."

17. "You do not get enough exercise," Sister Katrina says. "You go from your room to the convent and back again. Explore more. Go on. It won't hurt you. What you need, Rifka, is some fresh Belgian air."

18. "Please," I said again, beginning in Flemish, finishing in Yiddish. "I am very . . . lost."

19. "Listen to her, Marie," he crows. "Is she not wonderful?"

20. I don't have to sterilize every stitch of cloth that comes near my head. I don't have to look like a poor, needy immigrant Jew from Berdichev.

21. "Godspeed," he said. "Go ahead."

22. Maybe when I write and tell you how wonderful America is, you will change your mind and come too, bringing the rest of our family with you out of Russia. Then we will all be together again.

23. "All those sons and then a daughter . . . You are a treasure to your mama and papa. And to your brothers."

24. "You are such a brave girl, Rifka. And so clever to have managed on your own."

25. "Come . . . Quickly. You must stay down in the hold while the storm lasts."

26. "We lost one sailor overboard in the storm."

27. In Russia, all America meant to me was excitement, adventure. Now, coming to America means so much more. It is not simply a place you go when you run away. America is a place to begin anew."

28. "Why are you holding me? Why have you put me with these people? I don't belong here. I belong in America. I have come to America."

29. "You don't need hair to be a good wife, do you? Jewish women wear wigs all the time. I could wear a wig and still be a good wife."

30. "What's the matter with you? Why don't you eat?"

31. "What's the matter? You don't recognize your own sister?"

Quotations *Letters from Rifka*

32. "Why is such a great country like America afraid of a little Jewish girl just because she doesn't have nay hair on her head? The truth, Mama, is that they're afraid I will never find a husband. As if I need hair to get married."

33. "Look what you are doing, Ilya. You are going to get us killed. Look how you are wasting the paper."

34. "No, no Pushkin. I'm going to write a poem of my own."

35. "Read to them. Show them you are smart enough to live in America."

36. "He is my sister's son. Of course I want him. He is my flesh and blood. I sent for him to give him a better life here in America. I work day and night so he can have a good life."

37. "I have no doubt that if you wish to marry, you will do so, whether you have hair or not."

38. "Here, Rifka Nebrot. Welcome to America."

39. "Whatever it is, I'm certain it will go away." / "This isn't going away. Here, feel for yourself."

40. "Never mind the trouble, my sister Rifka is going to enter America in style."

Daily Lesson Plans *Letters from Rifka*

LESSON SIXTEEN

Objectives
1. To further explore Rifka's character
2. To show students the difference between writing a personal opinion essay and writing a persuasive letter
3. To evaluate students' writing

Activity #1

In Writing Assignment #1 students answered the question, "Why would you want to go to America?" In doing so, they wrote an essay expressing their personal opinions. In this assignment, students may use some of the same content but will use it to persuade someone else to come to America. Show students the difference in approach they will take in their writing considering the purpose of writing and the audience.

Activity #2

Distribute Writing Assignment #3. Discuss the directions in detail.

Activity #2

Allow ample time for students to complete the assignment. Tell student when the assignment will be due, and collect it at that time.

WRITING ASSIGNMENT #3 *Letters from Rifka*
Writing to Persuade

PROMPT
The book is a collection of letters from Rifka to her cousin, Tovah. At one point Rifka suggests that Tovah might want to come to America, too. Imagine that it is one year after Rifka has arrived in New York City. Now she is writing to Tovah to convince her to come to America and bring the rest of the family with her.

PREWRITING
Make a list of the things Rifka has done in the past year that she wants to tell Tovah, as well as a list of the reasons she thinks Tovah should come to America. Think of statements to support each of your reasons, and list them under each reason. Then number the reasons in order from most to least important.

DRAFTING
Have Rifka greet Tovah and let her know what has been happening for the past year. Then state the request to have Tovah move to America.

Use one paragraph for each reason that Rifka has for suggesting that Tovah move. Use the supporting statements for each reason.

Close your letter by asking Tovah to reply to you within a certain amount of time.

PEER CONFERENCING/REVISING
When you finish the rough draft of your persuasive letter, ask another student to read it. After reading your rough draft, the student should tell you what he/she liked best about your work, which parts were difficult to understand, and ways in which your work could be improved. Reread your text considering your critic's comments, and make the revisions you think are necessary.

PROOFREADING/EDITING
Do a final proofreading of your persuasive letter, double checking your grammar, spelling, organization, and the clarity of your ideas.

FINAL DRAFT
Follow your teacher's guidance for completing the final draft of your paper.

Daily Lesson Plans *Letters from Rifka*

LESSON SEVENTEEN

Objective
To review all of the vocabulary work done in this unit

VOCABULARY REVIEW ACTIVITIES

1. Divide your class into two teams and have an old-fashioned spelling or definition bee.

2. Give individuals or groups of students a *Letters from Rifka* Vocabulary Word Search Puzzle with a word list. The person (group) to find all of the vocabulary words in the puzzle first wins.

3. Give students a *Letters from Rifka* Vocabulary Word Search Puzzle without the word list. The person or group to find the most vocabulary words in the puzzle wins.

4. Put a *Letters from Rifka* Vocabulary Crossword Puzzle onto a transparency on the overhead projector and do the puzzle together as a class.

5. Give students a *Letters from Rifka* Vocabulary Matching Worksheet to do.

6. Use words from the word jumble page and have students spell them correctly, then use them in original sentences.

7. Have students write a story in which they correctly use as many vocabulary words as possible. Have students read their compositions orally. Post the most original compositions on your bulletin board.

8. Have students work in teams and play charades with the vocabulary words.

9. Select a word of the day and encourage students to use it correctly in their writing and speaking vocabulary.

Daily Lesson Plans *Letters from Rifka*

LESSON SEVENTEEN, continued

10. Have a contest to see which students can find the most vocabulary words used in other sources. You may want to have a bulletin board available so the students can write down their word, the sentence it was used in, and the source.

11. Assign a word to each student, or let them choose a word. Have them look up the origin of the word, the part of speech, definition, a synonym, and an antonym. Then have them write a sentence using the word. Have students present their information orally to the class.

LESSON EIGHTEEN

Objective
    To review the main events and ideas of *Letters from Rifka*

Activity #1
    Choose one of the review games/activities included in this packet and spend your class time as outlined there.

Activity #2
    Remind students of the date of the unit test. Stress the review of the study guides and their class notes as a last minute, brush-up review.

Daily Lesson Plans *Letters from Rifka*

REVIEW GAMES/ACTIVITIES *Letters from Rifka*

1. Ask the class to make up a unit test for *Letters from Rifka* (including a separate answer key). The test should have 4 sections: multiple choice, true/false, short answer, and essay. Students may use 1/2 period to make the test with a separate answer key and then swap papers and use the other 1/2 class period to take a test a classmate has devised. (open book) You may want to use the unit test included in this packet or take questions from the students' unit tests to formulate your own test.

2. Take 1/2 period for students to make up true and false questions (including the answers). Collect the papers, and divide the class into two teams. Draw a big tic-tac-toe board on the chalkboard. Make one team X and one team O. Ask questions to each side, giving each student one turn. If the question is answered correctly, that students' team's letter (X or O) is placed in the box. If the answer is incorrect, no mark is placed in the box. The object is to get three marks in a row like tic-tac-toe. You may want to keep track of the number of games won for each team.

3. Take 1/2 period for students to make up questions (true/false and short answer). Collect the questions. Divide the class into two teams. You'll alternate asking questions to individual members of teams A & B (like in a spelling bee). The question keeps going from A to B until it is correctly answered, then a new question is asked. A correct answer does not allow the team to get another question. Correct answers are +2 points; incorrect answers are -1 point.

4. Allow students time to quiz each other (in pairs or small groups) from their study guides and class notes.

5. Give students a *Letters from Rifka* crossword puzzle to complete.

6. Divide your class into two teams. Use the *Letters from Rifka* crossword words with their letters jumbled as a word list. Student 1 from Team A faces off against Student 1 from Team B. You write the first jumbled word on the board. The first student (1A or 1B) to unscramble the word wins the chance for his/her team to score points. If 1A wins the jumble, go to student 2A and give him/her a clue. He/she must give you the correct word which matches that clue. If he/she does, Team A scores a point, and you give student 3A a clue for which you expect another correct response. Continue giving Team A clues until some team member makes an incorrect response. An incorrect response sends the game back to the jumbled-word face off, this time with students 2A and 2B. Instead of repeating giving clues to the first few students of each team, continue with the student after the one who gave the last incorrect response on the team.

7. Take on the persona of "The Answer Person." Allow students to ask any question about the book. Answer the questions, or tell students where to look in the book to find the answer.

Unit Review Activities *Letters from Rifka*

8. Students may enjoy playing charades with events from the story. Select a student to start. Give him/her a card with a scene or event from the story. Allow the players to use their books to find the scene being described. The first person to guess each charade performs the next one.

9. Play a categories-type quiz game. (A master is included in this Unit Plan). Make an overhead transparency of the categories form. Divide the class into teams of three or four players each. Have each team Choose a recorder and a banker. Choose a team to go first. That team will choose a category and point amount. Ask the question to the entire class.(Use the Study Guide Quiz and Vocabulary questions.) Give the teams one minute to discuss the answer and write it down. Walk around the room and check the answers. Each team that answers correctly receives the points. (Incorrect answers are not penalized; they just don't receive any points). Cross out that square on the playing board. Play continues until all squares have been used. The winning team is the one with the most points. You can assign bonus points to any square or squares you choose.

10. Have individual students draw scenes from the book. Display the scenes and have the rest of the class look in their books to find the chapter or section that is being depicted. The first student to find the correct scene then displays his or her picture. When the game is over, collect the pictures and put them in a binder for students to look at during their free time.

NOTE: If students do not need the extra review, omit this lesson and go on to the test.

QUIZ GAME *Letters from Rifka*

September 2, 1919, Russia through October 5, 1919, Motziv, Poland	November 3, 1919, Motziv, Poland through December 1, 1919, Warsaw, Poland	February 25, 1920, Antwerp, Belgium through September 14, 1920, Antwerp, Belgium	September 16, 1920, Somewhere on the Atlantic Ocean through October 7, 1920, Ellis Island	October 9, 1920, Ellis Island through October 22, 1920, Ellis Island
100	100	100	100	100
200	200	200	200	200
300	300	300	300	300
400	400	400	400	400
500	500	500	500	500

Daily Lesson Plans *Letters from Rifka*

LESSON NINETEEN

Objective
To test the students understanding of the main ideas, themes, and events in *Letters from Rifka*

Activity #1
Distribute *Letters from Rifka* tests. Discuss the directions in detail and allow students the entire class period to complete the test. If they finish this segment early, they may continue to work on their "take home" essays (Writing Assignment #3) until the end of the period.

Activity #2
Collect all test papers and assigned books prior to the end of the period.

NOTES ABOUT THE UNIT TESTS IN THIS UNIT:

There are 5 different unit tests which follow.

There are two short answer tests which are based primarily on facts from the novel. The answer key for short answer unit test 1 follows the student test. The answer key for short answer test 2 follows the student short answer unit test 2.

There is one advanced short answer unit test. It is based on the extra discussion questions. Use the matching key for short answer unit test 2 to check the matching section of the advanced short answer unit test. There is no key for the short answer questions. The answers will be based on the discussions you have had during class.

There are two multiple choice unit tests. Following the two unit tests, you will find an answer sheet on which students should mark their answers. The same answer sheet should be used for both tests; however, students' answers will be different for each test. Following the students' answer sheet for the multiple choice tests you will find your two keys: one for multiple-choice test 1 and one for multiple-choice test 2.

The short answer tests have a vocabulary section. You should choose 10 of the vocabulary words from this unit, read them orally and have the students write them down. Then, either have students write a definition or use the words in sentences. The second part of the vocabulary test is matching.

Daily Lesson Plans *Letters from Rifka*

LESSON TWENTY

Objectives
1. To widen the breadth of students' knowledge about the topics discussed or touched upon in *Letters from Rifka*
2. To present the nonfiction assignments

Activity #1

Ask each student to give a brief oral report about the nonfiction work he/she read for the nonfiction assignment. Your criteria for evaluating this report will vary depending on the level of your students. You may wish for students to give the complete report without using notes of any kind. Or you may want students to read directly from a written report. You may want to do something between these two options. Make students aware of your criteria in ample time for them to prepare their reports.

Start with one student's report. After that, ask if anyone else in the class has read on a topic related to the first student's report. If no one has, choose another student at random. After each report, be sure to ask if anyone has a report related to the one just completed. That will help keep continuity during the discussion of the reports.

Activity #2

Collect the students' written reports. Put them in a binder and have the binder available for students to read.

Activity #3

If the class or school has a Web site, post the nonfiction reports there.

UNIT TESTS

SHORT ANSWER UNIT TEST 1, *Letters from Rifka*

I. Matching/Identification
Directions: Place the letter of the matching definition on the blank line.

_____ 1. banana   A. hours passengers stay in steerage during storm

_____ 2. chocolate   B. Ilya's age

_____ 3. ice cream   C. street seller takes all of Rifka's money for one

_____ 4. orange   D. Rifka's age when she left Russia

_____ 5. thirty-six (36) E. Saul is surprised that Rifka knows what it is

_____ 6. seven (7)   F. number of brothers that Rifka has

_____ 7. twelve (12)   G. years ago when Rifka's older brothers left

_____ 8. five (5)   H. Rifka gets it in Antwerp from a man with a cart

_____ 9. fourteen (14)   I. age of Russian peasant girl

_____ 10. sixteen (16)   J. Rifka describes it as "biting off a corner of heaven"

Short Answer Unit Test 1, *Letters From Rifka*
II. Short Answer
Directions: Answer each question.

1. Where are Rifka and her family going, how do they plan to get there? Why is the family going on this journey?

2. Describe the family's treatment at the Polish border. How does Rifka react to this?

3. What does the doctor at the steamship say about Rifka? What does Rifka realize when he says this?

4. What is the HIAS? How does it help Rifka and her family?

5. What compliment does Sister Katrina give Rifka? What is Rifka's thought about the compliment that she writes to Tovah?

Short Answer Unit Test 1, *Letters From Rifka*

6. How does Rifka describe what America meant to her in Russia? How does she describe what it means as she is sailing into New York?

7. Explain what the doctors mean when they tell Rifka the American government may view her as a "social responsibility." Include her response.

8. When Mama visits the hospital, she watches Rifka doing her jobs. What does she say about this?

9. What "trouble" do Ilya and Rifka get into? Why is Rifka frightened? What is Nurse Bowen's response when Rifka tells her about it?

10. As they prepare to leave Ellis Island, Saul tells Rifka there are gifts waiting at home. What are they?

Short Answer Unit Test 1, *Letters from Rifka*

III. Quotations
Directions: Identify the speaker and discuss the significance of each quotation.

1. "You must say nothing about the nature of her illness to anyone. Not even to your cousin. As for the child, she will probably die. Most do. That's how it goes with typhus."

2. "Why would you want to go to America? You can do everything you want right here. I would never leave Poland."

3. "If I can't go to America, please send me back to Berdichev."

4. "You can distract the guards, can't you, little sister?"

5. "Please. I am very . . . lost."

Short Answer Unit Test 1, *Letters from Rifka*

IV: Essay
    Discuss Rifka's growth during her ordeal. Use examples from the novel to support your answer.

Short Answer Unit Test 1, *Letters from Rifka*

V. Vocabulary Part 1
   Listen to the vocabulary word and spell it. After you have spelled all the words, go back and write down the definitions.

WORD	DEFINITION
1. _____	_____
2. _____	_____
3. _____	_____
4. _____	_____
5. _____	_____
6. _____	_____
7. _____	_____
8. _____	_____
9. _____	_____
10. _____	_____

Vocabulary Part 2: Place the letter of the matching definition on the blank line.

_____ 1. advantage   A. removal of a foreigner from a country
_____ 2. compassion   B. action taken to protect against harm
_____ 3. deportation   C. slanted; leaning at an angle
_____ 4. intentions   D. a piece of fabric worn over the shoulders
_____ 5. precaution   E. a foul, disgusting smell
_____ 6. shawl   F. intelligence; common sense
_____ 7. stench   G. a severe storm with strong winds and rain
_____ 8. tempest   H. a favorable position
_____ 9. tilted   I. plans; purposes
_____ 10. wits   J. kindness; consideration

ANSWER KEY: SHORT ANSWER UNIT TEST I *Letters from Rifka*

I. Matching/Identification
Directions: Place the letter of the matching definition on the blank line.

E	1. banana	A.	number of hours passengers stay in steerage during storm
J	2. chocolate	B.	Ilya's age
H	3. ice cream	C.	street seller takes all of Rifka's money for one
C	4. orange	D.	Rifka's age when she left Russia
A	5. thirty-six	E.	Saul is surprised that Rifka knows what it is
B	6. seven	F.	number of brothers that Rifka has
D	7. twelve	G.	years ago when Rifka's older brothers left
F	8. five	H.	Rifka gets it in Antwerp from a man with a cart
G	9. fourteen	I.	age of Russian peasant girl
I	10. sixteen	J.	Rifka describes it as "biting off a corner of heaven"

II. Short Answer
Directions: Answer each question.

1. Where are Rifka and her family going, how do they plan to get there? Why is the family going on this journey?
    They are planning to leave Russia by train, go into Poland, and from there they want to go to America. Rifka's older brother Nathan has already been taken into the Russian and now her brother Saul is about to be taken. Rifka's parents have planned for this time to escape and live with their older sons, who have already moved to America.

2. Describe the family's treatment at the Polish border. How does Rifka react to this?
    The family is ordered to get off the train at the border. Guards search them and order them to remove their clothes so the doctor can check them for diseases. Their bodies, clothes, and possessions are fumigated. Rifka says the doctor made her feel dirty.

3. What does the doctor at the steamship say about Rifka? What does Rifka realize when he says this?
    He says that Rifka has ringworm and cannot go on the ship. The treatment will take many months. Rifka realizes that the girl on the train had ringworm and that's where she got it.

Answer Key Short Answer Unit Test 1, *Letters from Rifka*

4. What is the HIAS? How does it help Rifka and her family?
    The HIAS is the Hebrew Immigration Aid Society. They help Jews with immigration and other problems. One of the workers in Warsaw arranges for Rifka to go to Antwerp, Belgium and live with a family while she gets treatment at a hospital for the ringworm.

5. What compliment does Sister Katrina give Rifka? What is Rifka's thought about the compliment that she writes to Tovah?
    Sister Katrina tells Rifka she is clever. Rifka writes that Tovah would like hearing that someone thinks she (Rifka) is clever.

6. How does Rifka describe what America meant to her in Russia? How does she describe what it means as she is sailing into New York?
    In Russia she thinks America is excitement and adventure. Now it is a place to start over. She thinks life can be good in America for a clever girl.

7. Explain what the doctors mean when they tell Rifka the American government may view her as a "social responsibility." Include her response.
    Since she is bald, she may never find a husband. Then the government will have to take care of her. Rifka says she does not need hair to be a good wife. Also, according to Jewish law a woman may shave her head. She thinks that in America, looks are more important than wits.

8. When Mama visits the hospital, she watches Rifka doing her jobs. What does she say about this?
    Mama says Rifka is like her father, who knows how to heal people. Mama also admires the way Rifka is learning English.

9. What "trouble" do Ilya and Rifka get into? Why is Rifka frightened? What is Nurse Bowen's response when Rifka tells her about it?
    Ilya unrolls a roll of toilet paper. Rifka is upset because in Russia it is a crime to waste paper. She thinks they will get killed or sent back to Russia. Nurse Bowen laughs and says it is not a crime to waste paper in America. There is plenty of paper.

10. As they prepare to leave Ellis Island, Saul tells Rifka there are gifts waiting at home. What are they?
    There are new candlesticks for Mama and paper for Rifka.

Answer Key Short Answer Unit Test 1, *Letters from Rifka*

III. Quotations
Directions: Identify the speaker and discuss the significance of each quotation.

1. "You must say nothing about the nature of her illness to anyone," the medical student told Papa. "Not even to your cousin. As for the child, she will probably die. Most do. That's how it goes with typhus."
    The medical student in Motziv, Poland said this to Rifka's parents. He had examined Rifka and told them she had typhus.

2. She said, "Why would you want to go to America? You can do everything you want right here. I would never leave Poland."
    The young peasant girl on the train from Motziv to Warsaw said this to Rifka when Rifka told the girl she and her family were going to America.

3. I said, "If I can't go to America, please send me back to Berdichev."
    Rifka said this to the HIAS worker when she told the family that Rifka should go to Antwerp alone to get treatment for the ringworm. Papa reminded Rifka that if she went back the Russians would kill her and it would also put the family members who were still in Berdichev in danger.

4. "You can distract the guards, can't you, little sister?"
    Nathan said this to Rifka. The family was at the train station preparing to sneak about the train. Rifka's job was to distract the guards while the family got on the train.

5. "Please," I said again, beginning in Flemish, finishing in Yiddish. "I am very . . . lost."
    Rifka said this to the milkman. She was exploring Antwerp by herself and got lost. He took her all the way home.

IV: Essay
    Discuss Rifka's growth during the novel. Use examples from the novel to support your answer.

(For teacher notes)

Short Answer Unit Test 1, *Letters from Rifka*

V. Vocabulary Part 1
   Use this space to write the words and definitions you have chosen for this test.

   WORD   DEFINITION

1. _____   _____

2. _____   _____

3. _____   _____

4. _____   _____

5. _____   _____

6. _____   _____

7. _____   _____

8. _____   _____

9. _____   _____

10. _____   _____

Vocabulary Part 2: Place the letter of the matching definition on the blank line.

H	1. advantage	A. removal of a foreigner from a country
J	2. compassion	B. action taken to protect against harm
A	3. deportation	C. slanted; leaning at an angle
I	4. intentions	D. a piece of fabric worn over the shoulders
B	5. precaution	E. a foul, disgusting smell
D	6. shawl	F. intelligence; common sense
E	7. stench	G. a severe storm with strong winds and rain
G	8. tempest	H. a favorable position
C	9. tilted	I. plans; purposes
F	10. wits	J. kindness; consideration

SHORT ANSWER UNIT TEST 2, *Letters from Rifka*

I. Matching/Identification
Directions: Place the letter of the matching definition on the blank line.

_____ 1. Antwerp   A. Rifka's native language

_____ 2. Berdichev   B. Rifka speaks it without an accent

_____ 3. Ellis Island   C. city in Belgium where Rifka stays for treatment

_____ 4. Motziv   D. Rifka learns it in Motziv

_____ 5. New York   E. language Rifka learns in Antwerp

_____ 6. Warsaw   F. family's home city in Ukraine, Russia

_____ 7. Yiddish   G. family leaves for America from here

_____ 8. Russian   H. Polish city where family stayed during typhus illness

_____ 9. Polish   I. Rifka must stay in hospital there

_____ 10. Flemish   J. family moves to this American city

Short Answer Unit Test 2, *Letters From Rifka*
II. Short Answer
Directions: Answer each question.

1. What is Rifka's job as the family is getting ready to go and why does she have to do this? How does she go about doing the job, and who helps her?

2. Describe Rifka's meeting with the peasant girl on the train. Include what the girl looked like, the language she spoke, and what Rifka did for her. What happens to Rifka as a result of her actions?

3. In Warsaw, one of the HIAS workers makes a suggestion to Rifka and her parents. What is Rifka's response to the worker's suggestion? What is her father's response? What does Rifka do? How does she describe herself?

4. What does Rifka think of Antwerp? Include her thoughts about the people, the scenery, and the food. What foods does she discover and what does she think of them?

5. Briefly describe the storm at sea. Tell what Rifka does and how she feels. Tell how long the storm lasts. What happens to Pieter during the storm? How does Rifka feel about it? . Describe what Rifka does after the storm is over, and after she finds out about Pieter. Include how she feels.

Short Answer Unit Test 2, *Letters From Rifka*

6. Why does Rifka dislike Ilya at first? Why does she feed Ilya? How does she feel about her actions?

7. Describe what each of the Nebrot family members is doing for work in New York.

8. What does Rifka ask Nurse Bowen to give her? What does she do with it? How does she feel about it?

9. What action does Ilya take that helps with Mr. Fargate's decision about Rifka entering the United States?

10. What does Rifka discover when her kerchief falls off at the hearing?

Short Answer Unit Test 2, *Letters from Rifka*

III. Quotations
Directions: Identify the speaker and discuss the significance of each quotation.

1. "Thief! Give me back my food!"

2. "So they stole our candlesticks. It could be worse, Rifka, much worse. Stop sniffling and finish getting dressed."

3. "No, I am sorry. Your daughter cannot join you. Our company will not sell her passage to America."

4. "Tovah, I am like an orphan now."

5. "Never mind the trouble, my sister Rifka is going to enter America in style."

Short Answer Unit Test 2, *Letters from Rifka*

IV: Essay

Are the characters in *Letters from Rifka* stereotypes? If so, explain which ones are stereotypes and the usefulness of employing stereotypes in *Letters from Rifka*. If they are not, explain how they merit individuality.

Short Answer Unit Test 2, *Letters from Rifka*

V. Vocabulary Part 1
　　　Listen to the vocabulary word and spell it. After you have spelled all the words, go back and write down the definitions.

　　　WORD　　　　　　　　　　　　　　　DEFINITION

1. _____　　_____

2. _____　　_____

3. _____　　_____

4. _____　　_____

5. _____　　_____

6. _____　　_____

7. _____　　_____

8. _____　　_____

9. _____　　_____

10. _____　　_____

Vocabulary Part 2: Place the letter of the matching definition on the blank line.

_____ 1. billowing　　　　A. not strong; easily broken
_____ 2. contagious　　　 B. a treatment to get rid of bugs or disease
_____ 3. fragile　　　　　C. put something away for future use
_____ 4. fumigation　　　 D. a hospital room for several patients
_____ 5. monitor　　　　　E. action taken to protect against harm
_____ 6. precaution　　　 F. inflicted pain or discomfort
_____ 7. precious　　　　 G. rolling or flowing upward
_____ 8. stow　　　　　　 H. much loved and valued
_____ 9. tormented　　　　I. spread from one person to another
_____ 10. ward　　　　　　J. watch over; check on

ANSWER KEY: SHORT ANSWER UNIT TEST 2, *Letters from Rifka*

I. Matching/Identification

C	1. Antwerp	A.	Rifka's native language
F	2. Berdichev	B.	Rifka speaks it without an accent
I	3. Ellis Island	C.	city in Belgium where Rifka stays for treatment
H	4. Motziv	D.	Rifka learns it in Motziv
J	5. New York	E.	language Rifka learns in Antwerp
G	6. Warsaw	F.	family's home city in Ukraine, Russia
A	7. Yiddish	G.	family leaves for America from here
B	8. Russian	H.	Polish city where family stayed during typhus illness
D	9. Polish	I.	Rifka must stay in hospital there
E	10. Flemish	J.	family moves to this American city

II. Short Answer

1. What is Rifka's job as the family is getting ready to go and why does she have to do this? How does she go about doing the job, and who helps her?

    Rifka distracts the guards at the train station so they don't search the boxcars and find her other family members. She is the only one in the family with blond hair, so she looks Russian. She also speaks Russian without a Yiddish accent. She talks to the guards and has mostly distracted them. Her Uncle Avrum asks them for help, saying someone has broken into his factory. Since Avrum is a respected businessman, the guards have to help him. They go with him and the train leaves.

2. Describe Rifka's meeting with the peasant girl on the train. Include what the girl looked like, the language she spoke, and what Rifka did for her. What happens to Rifka as a result of her actions?

    The girl was about sixteen and spoke Polish. She was nursing a little baby. She had oily hair with sores on her scalp. Rifka offered to braid the girl's hair and she accepted. Later, when Rifka goes to the steamship company with her family to buy tickets to America, the doctor says that Rifka has ringworm and cannot go on the ship. The treatment will take many months. Rifka realizes that the girl on the train had ringworm and that's where she got it.

Answer Key Short Answer Unit Test 2, *Letters from Rifka*

3. In Warsaw, one of the HIAS workers makes a suggestion to Rifka and her parents. What is Rifka's response to the worker's suggestion? What is her father's response? What does Rifka do? How does she describe herself?

    One of the workers in Warsaw arranges for Rifka to go to Antwerp, Belgium and live with a family while she gets treatment at a hospital for the ringworm. Rifka says she would rather go back to Berdichev. Her father reminds her that the Russians are angry at the family because her five brothers escaped service in the Army. If she goes back she will be killed. Rifka agrees to go to Antwerp. She says she is like an orphan.

4. What does Rifka think of Antwerp? Include her thoughts about the people, the scenery, and the food. What foods does she discover and what does she think of them?

    She thinks Antwerp is wonderful. The people are friendly and kind, the food is splendid, and the scenery is wonderful. She discovers ice cream and chocolate and thinks they are wonderful.

5. Briefly describe the storm at sea. Tell what Rifka does and how she feels. Tell how long the storm lasts. What happens to Pieter during the storm? How does Rifka feel about it? Describe what Rifka does after the storm is over, and after she finds out about Pieter. Include how she feels.

    The storm starts at night and the force of it throws her on the floor. She goes on deck, where she is sick. Pieter moves her away from the side of the ship. He saves her from being pulled overboard by a wave. Then he takes her to steerage to be safe. The passengers stay in steerage for thirty-six hours. He washes overboard. When Rifka finds out, she feels like she is smothering. She cannot see or hear. Rifka cries until she cannot cry anymore. She feels how defenseless all people, not just Jews, are.

6. Why does Rifka dislike Ilya at first? Why does she feed Ilya? How does she feel about her actions?

    She dislikes him because he is a Russian peasant. If they were both in Russia, it would be his people killing hers. But she sees that he is just a scared little boy. She encourages him to eat and then feels very good about it.

7. Describe what each of the Nebrot family members is doing for work in New York.

    Mama and Papa are working in a clothing factory. Nathan works in a bakery. Saul goes to school. Isaac married a girl named Sadie Chenowitz, whose family is also from Berdichev. They have a baby boy named Aaron.

8. What does Rifka ask Nurse Bowen to give her? What does she do with it? How does she feel about it?

    She asks Nurse Bowen for some paper. She begins writing her own poems on the paper. She is happy to be writing. The writing comforts her. She thinks she is clever to be a poet.

9. What action does Ilya take that helps with Mr. Fargate's decision about Rifka entering the United States?

    Ilya recites one of Rifka's poems from memory. Mr. Fargate is impressed and says she may enter the country.

Answer Key Short Answer Unit Test 2, *Letters from Rifka*

10. What does Rifka discover when her kerchief falls off at the hearing?
    She discovers that she has some hair growing back.

III. Quotations

1. "Thief!" I cried in Russian. "Give me back my food!"
    Rifka said this to the innkeeper's daughter in Motziv. Rifka had hidden a portion of her herring and roll for Saul. Instead, the girl found it and ate it.

2. "So they stole our candlesticks," Mama said. "It could be worse, Rifka, much worse. Stop sniffling and finish getting dressed."
    The family had been stopped when the train arrived in Poland. They had all been told to remove their clothes and had been inspected by the doctor. In the meantime, guards had inspected their belongings and had taken Mama's candlesticks from Rifka's rucksack. Rifka was upset when she discovered they were missing.

3. "No," the doctor said. "I am sorry. Your daughter cannot join you. Our company will not sell her passage to America."
    The doctor in Warsaw said this to the Nebrots. The doctor had discovered that Rifka had ringworm. He would not allow her to go to America with her family.

4. "Tovah, I am like an orphan now."
    Rifka wrote this to Tovah after she (Rifka) had agreed to go to Antwerp alone to get treatment for the ringworm.

5. "Never mind the trouble, my sister Rifka is going to enter America in style."
    Rifka's brother Isaac said this. The family had gathered at the hospital on Ellis Island for Rifka's entry hearing. Mr. Fargate had just signed her papers saying she was allowed to enter America.

IV: Essay

Are the characters in *Letters from Rifka* stereotypes? If so, explain which ones are stereotypes and the usefulness of employing stereotypes in *Letters from Rifka*. If they are not, explain how they merit individuality.

(for teacher notes)

Answer Key Short Answer Unit Test 2, *Letters from Rifka*

V. Vocabulary Part 1
Use this space to write down the words and definitions you have chosen for this test.

	WORD	DEFINITION
1.	_____	_____
2.	_____	_____
3.	_____	_____
4.	_____	_____
5.	_____	_____
6.	_____	_____
7.	_____	_____
8.	_____	_____
9.	_____	_____
10.	_____	_____

Vocabulary Part 2: Place the letter of the matching definition on the blank line.

G 1. billowing   A. not strong; easily broken
I 2. contagious   B. a treatment to get rid of bugs or disease
A 3. fragile   C. put something away for future use
B 4. fumigation   D. a hospital room for several patients
J 5. monitor   E. action taken to protect against harm
E 6. precaution   F. inflicted pain or discomfort
H 7. precious   G. rolling or flowing upward
C 8. stow   H. much loved and valued
F 9. tormented   I. spread from one person to another
D 10. ward   J. watch over; check on

Advanced Short Answer Unit Test, *Letters from Rifka*

I. Matching/Identification
Directions: Place the letter of the matching definition on the blank line.

_____ 1. Antwerp   A. Rifka's native language

_____ 2. Berdichev   B. Rifka speaks it without an accent

_____ 3. Ellis Island   C. city in Belgium where Rifka stays for treatment

_____ 4. Motziv   D. Rifka learns it in Motziv

_____ 5. New York   E. language Rifka learns in Antwerp

_____ 6. Warsaw   F. family's home city in Ukraine, Russia

_____ 7. Yiddish   G. family leaves for America from here

_____ 8. Russian   H. Polish city where family stayed during typhus illness

_____ 9. Polish   I. Rifka must stay in hospital there

_____ 10. Flemish   J. family moves to this American city

II. Short Answer

1. Discuss Rifka's growth during her ordeal. Use examples from the novel to support your answer.

2. What are the main conflicts in the novel? How are they resolved?

Advanced Short Answer Unit Test, *Letters from Rifka*

II. Short Answer, continued

3. Discuss the imagery used in the book. How vivid is it? How effective is it?

4. Are the characters in *Letters from Rifka* stereotypes? If so, explain which ones are stereotypes and the usefulness of employing stereotypes in *Letters from Rifka*. If they are not, explain how they merit individuality.

5. Did the quotes from Pushkin add to your understanding of Rifka as a character? If so, explain how. If not, explain why not.

Advanced Short Answer Unit Test, *Letters from Rifka*

III. Quotations
Directions: Identify the speaker and discuss the significance of each quotation.

1. "I'm here to take the train. My mother has found me work in a wealthy house."

2. "So they stole our candlesticks . . ." It could be worse, much worse. Stop sniffling and finish getting dressed."

3. "No. I am sorry. Your daughter cannot join you. Our company will not sell her passage to America.

4. "Why are you holding me? Why have you put me with these people? I don't belong here. I belong in America. I have come to America."

5. "Read to them. Show them you are smart enough to live in America."

Advanced Short Answer Unit Test *Letters from Rifka*

<u>III. Quotations, continued</u>

6. "Please," . . . I am very . . . lost."

7. "There you are! Thief! You steal my oranges! Help! Police! What monster are you, that you steal from an old man!"/ "I did not! I paid you. You took all the money I had!"

8. "He is my sister's son. Of course I want him. He is my flesh and blood. I sent for him to give him a better life here in America. I work day and night so he can have a good life."

9. "I have no doubt that if you wish to marry, you will do so, whether you have hair or not."

10. "Never mind the trouble, my sister . . . is going to enter America in style."

Advanced Short Answer Unit Test *Letters from Rifka*

IV. Vocabulary

Directions: Listen to the words and write them down. After you have written down all of the words, write a paragraph in which you use all the words. The paragraph must in some way relate to the book *Letters from Rifka*.

MULTIPLE CHOICE UNIT TEST 1 *Letters from Rifka*

I. Matching/Identification:
Directions: Match the term and its meaning.

1. banana   A. hours passengers stay in steerage during storm

2. chocolate   B. Ilya's age

3. ice cream   C. street seller takes all of Rifka's money for one

4. orange   D. Rifka's age when she left Russia

5. thirty-six (36)   E. Saul is surprised that Rifka knows what it is

6. seven (7)   F. number of brothers that Rifka has

7. twelve (12)   G. years ago when Rifka's older brothers left

8. five (5)   H. Rifka gets it in Antwerp from a man with a cart

9. fourteen (14)   I. age of Russian peasant girl

10. sixteen (16)   J. Rifka describes it as "biting off a corner of heaven"

Multiple Choice Unit Test 1 *Letters from Rifka*

II. Multiple Choice

1. True or False: Rifka and her family are planning to go to America.
    A. True
    B. False

2. The treatment of the doctor at the Polish border makes Rifka feel _____.
    A. happy
    B. worried
    C. relieved
    D. dirty

3. At the steamship office, Rifka realizes that she got ____ from the peasant girl.
    A. shingles
    B. ringworm
    C. measles
    D. polio

4. One of the HIAS workers arranges for Rifka to go to _____ and live with a family while she gets treatment at a hospital for the ringworm.
    A. Antwerp, Belgium
    B. Paris, France
    C. Rome, Italy
    D. Berlin, Germany

5. Sister Katrina tells Rifka she is _____.
    A. brave
    B. thoughtful
    C. clever
    D. funny

6. Rifka thinks America is a place to _____.
    A. start over
    B. get rich
    C. eat chocolate
    D. buy pretty clothes

7. The government thinks Rifka may become a _____.
    A. high-school dropout
    B. juvenile delinquent
    C. social responsibility
    D. missing person

Multiple Choice Unit Test 1 *Letters from Rifka*

8. Mama says Rifka is like her ____, who knows how to heal people.
    A. cousin
    B. sister
    C. father
    D. uncle

9. What "trouble" do Ilya and Rifka get into?
    A. They take two extra glasses of milk.
    B. Ilya unrolls a roll of toilet paper.
    C. They use a dinner tray to sled in the hallway.
    D. They throw a ball and break a window.

10. Saul tells Rifka there are gifts waiting at home. What are they?
    A. There is a prayer shawl for Papa and a toy for the baby.
    B. There are schoolbooks and clothes for Rifka.
    C. There is chocolate and ice cream for everyone.
    D. There are new candlesticks for Mama and paper for Rifka.

Multiple Choice Unit Test 1 *Letters from Rifka*

III. Quotations
Directions: Match the two parts of each quotation.

1. "As for the child, she will probably die.

2. "Why would you want to go to America?

3. "If I can't go to America,

4. "You can distract the guards,

5. "Please,

6. "Why are you holding me? Why have you put me with these people?

7. "What's the matter with you?

8. "I have no doubt that if you wish to marry,

9. "This isn't going away.

10. "Look what you are doing, Ilya.

A. please send me back to Berdichev."

B. Why don't you eat?"

C. You can do everything you want right here. I would never leave Poland."

D. Here, feel for yourself."

E. you will do so, whether you have hair or not."

F. Most do. That's how it goes with typhus."

G. You are going to get us killed. Look how you are wasting the paper."

H. I am very . . . lost."

I. I don't belong here. I belong in America. I have come to America."

J. can't you, little sister?"

Multiple Choice Unit Test 1 *Letters from Rifka*

IV. Vocabulary Part I Directions: Match the word and its meaning.

_____ 1. advantage   A. removal of a foreigner from a country
_____ 2. compassion   B. action taken to protect against harm
_____ 3. deportation   C. slanted; leaning at an angle
_____ 4. intentions   D. a piece of fabric worn over the shoulders
_____ 5. precaution   E. a foul, disgusting smell
_____ 6. shawl   F. intelligence; common sense
_____ 7. stench   G. a severe storm with strong winds and rain
_____ 8. tempest   H. a favorable position
_____ 9. tilted   I. plans; purposes
_____ 10. wits   J. kindness; consideration

Vocabulary Part 2 Directions: Mark the letter next to the word that matches the definition.

11. inflict pain or discomfort
    A. waxed
    B. skipped
    C. tormented
    D. huddled

12. want something a lot
    A. distract
    B. deny
    C. ache
    D. monitor

13. a small metal case that holds a picture
    A. sprout
    B. locket
    C. balcony
    D. herring

14. a child whose parents are dead
    A. distress
    B. margin
    C. orphan
    D. cousin

15. smart; intelligent
    A. gloom
    B. wistful
    C. clever
    D. idle

16. harmless misbehavior; naughtiness
    A. fury
    B. luxury
    C. advantage
    D. mischief

17. sections of a piece of writing
    A. lounges
    B. passages
    C. offenses
    D. rucksack

18. rolling or flowing upward
    A. trembling
    B. stricken
    C. odd
    D. billowing

19. spread from one person to another
    A. contagious
    B. tousle
    C. plunge
    D. evade

20. a hospital room for several patients
    A. ward
    B. typhus
    C. slumber
    D. exile

MULTIPLE CHOICE UNIT TEST 2 *Letters from Rifka*

I. Matching/Identification:
Directions: Match the term and its meaning.

1. Antwerp   A. Rifka's native language

2. Berdichev   B. Rifka speaks it without an accent

3. Ellis Island   C. city in Belgium where Rifka stays for treatment

4. Motziv   D. Rifka learns it in Motziv

5. New York   E. language Rifka learns in Antwerp

6. Warsaw   F. family's home city in Ukraine, Russia

7. Yiddish   G. family leaves for America from here

8. Russian   H. Polish city where family stayed during typhus illness

9. Polish   I. Rifka must stay in hospital there

10. Flemish   J. family moves to this American city

Multiple Choice Unit Test 2 *Letters from Rifka*

II. Multiple Choice

1. What is Rifka's job as the family is getting ready to go on their journey?
    A. Rifka distracts the guards at the train station.
    B. Rifka goes into town to buy food and other supplies.
    C. Rifka buys the train tickets.
    D. Rifka crawls through the cars looking for the best place to hide.

2. At the steamship office, Rifka realizes that she got ____ from the peasant girl.
    A. shingles
    B. ringworm
    C. measles
    D. polio

3. Rifka agrees to go for treatment in Antwerp, but says she is like _____.
    A. a terminally ill patient
    B. a helpless baby
    C. an orphan
    D. an old woman

4. In Antwerp, Rifka discovers _____ and thinks they are wonderful.
    A. ice cream and chocolate
    B. pizza and soda
    C. movies and popcorn
    D. TV and radio

5. When Rifka finds out that her friend Pieter washed overboard during the storm, she _____.
    A. tries to jump overboard herself
    B. feels like she is smothering
    C. faints on the deck
    D. laughs hysterically

6. Rifka feels good about her actions when she encourages Ilya to _____.
    A. hug her
    B. sleep
    C. pray
    D. eat

7. In New York City, Mama and Papa are working in _____.
    A. a clothing factory
    B. a bakery
    C. a hospital
    D. a subway station

Multiple Choice Unit Test 2 *Letters from Rifka*

8. Rifka begins to _____, which comforts her.
    A. play the guitar
    B. study nursing
    C. knit baby blankets
    D. write her own poems

9. What action does Ilya take that helps with Mr. Fargate's decision to let Rifka enter the United States?
    A. Ilya asks Mr. Fargate in perfect English.
    B. He says he will not leave without Rifka.
    C. Ilya recites one of Rifka's poems from memory.
    D. He offers to work to pay for her treatment.

10. True or False: During the hearings, Rifka discovers that the ringworm has returned.
    A. True
    B. False

Multiple Choice Unit Test 2 *Letters from Rifka*

III. Quotations
Directions: Match the two parts of each quotation.

1. "Nathan

2. Why is it that if a Russian peasant does not get what he wants,

3. As for the child,

4. "If I can't go to America,

5. I don't have to

6. You are a treasure

7. Never mind the trouble,

8. "I have no doubt that

9. "No, no Pushkin.

10. "What's the matter with you?

A. he feels justified in stealing it from a Jew?

B. please send me back to Berdichev."

C. to your mama and papa. And to your brothers."

D. if you wish to marry, you will do so, whether you have hair or not."

E. Why don't you eat?"

F. isn't going to return. Hurry! We must pack!"

G. I'm going to write a poem of my own."

H. sterilize every stitch of cloth that comes near my head.

I. my sister Rifka is going to enter America in style."

J. she will probably die. Most do. That's how it goes with typhus."

130

Multiple Choice Unit Test 2 *Letters from Rifka*

IV. Vocabulary Part I Directions: Match the word and its meaning.
1. billowing   A. not strong; easily broken
2. contagious   B. a treatment to get rid of bugs or disease
3. fragile   C. put something away for future use
4. fumigation   D. a hospital room for several patients
5. monitor   E. action taken to protect against harm
6. precaution   F. inflicted pain or discomfort
7. precious   G. rolling or flowing upward
8. stow   H. much loved and valued
9. tormented   I. spread from one person to another
10. ward   J. watch over; check on

Vocabulary Part 2 Directions: Mark the letter next to the word that matches the definition.

11. want something a lot
    A. distract
    B. deny
    C. ache
    D. monitor

12. holding tightly
    A. ache
    B. clasping
    C. distract
    D. drifting

13. an elegant room in a private home
    A. border
    B. salon
    C. tangle
    D. steerage

14. grow quickly
    A. tousle
    B. commit
    C. shatter
    D. sprout

15. full of uncontrolled anger or excitement
    A. numb
    B. practical
    C. frenzied
    D. odd

16. plans; purposes
    A. tempests
    B. intentions
    C. shawls
    D. peasants

17. a favorable position
    A. stench
    B. slumber
    C. advantage
    D. huddle

18. move around in a sneaky way
    A. slip
    B. blur
    C. plunge
    D. prowl

19. bent close to the ground
    A. crouched
    B. delicate
    C. mischief
    D. squeezed

20. tangle or mess up hair
    A. lurch
    B. tousle
    C. clasp
    D. cure

ANSWER SHEET MULTIPLE CHOICE UNIT TESTS *Letters from Rifka*

I. Matching	III. Quotations	IV. Vocabulary
1.	1.	1.
2.	2.	2.
3.	3.	3.
4.	4.	4.
5.	5.	5.
6.	6.	6.
7.	7.	7.
8.	8.	8.
9.	9.	9.
10.	10.	10.
		11.
II. Multiple Choice		12.
1. (A) (B) (C) (D)		13.
2. (A) (B) (C) (D)		14.
3. (A) (B) (C) (D)		15.
4. (A) (B) (C) (D)		16.
5. (A) (B) (C) (D)		17.
6. (A) (B) (C) (D)		18.
7. (A) (B) (C) (D)		19.
8. (A) (B) (C) (D)		20.
9. (A) (B) (C) (D)		
10. (A) (B) (C) (D)		

ANSWER SHEET KEY MULTIPLE CHOICE UNIT TEST 1 *Letters from Rifka*

I. Matching	III. Quotations	IV. Vocabulary
1. E	1. F	1. H
2. J	2. C	2. J
3. H	3. A	3. A
4. C	4. J	4. I
5. A	5. H	5. B
6. B	6. I	6. D
7. D	7. B	7. E
8. F	8. E	8. G
9. G	9. D	9. C
10. I	10. G	10. F
		11. C

II. Multiple Choice

1. ( ) (B) ( ) (D)
2. (A) (B) (C) ( )
3. (A) ( ) (C) (D)
4. ( ) (B) (C) (D)
5. (A) (B) ( ) (D)
6. ( ) (B) (C) (D)
7. (A) (B) ( ) (D)
8. (A) (B) ( ) (D)
9. (A) ( ) (C) (D)
10. (A) (B) (C) ( )

12. C
13. B
14. C
15. C
16. D
17. B
18. D
19. A
20. A

ANSWER SHEET KEY MULTIPLE CHOICE UNIT TEST 2 *Letters from Rifka*

I. Matching	III. Quotations	IV. Vocabulary
1. C	1. F	1. G
2. F	2. A	2. I
3. I	3. J	3. A
4. H	4. B	4. B
5. J	5. H	5. J
6. G	6. C	6. E
7. A	7. I	7. H
8. B	8. D	8. C
9. D	9. G	9. F
10. E	10. E	10. D
		11. C
II. Multiple Choice		12. B
1. ( ) (B) (C) (D)		13. B
2. (A) ( ) (C) (D)		14. D
3. (A) (B) ( ) (D)		15. C
4. ( ) (B) (C) (D)		16. B
5. (A) ( ) (C) (D)		17. C
6. (A) (B) (C) ( )		18. D
7. ( ) (B) (C) (D)		19. A
8. (A) (B) (C) ( )		20. B
9. (A) (B) ( ) (D)		
10. (A) ( ) (C) (D)		

UNIT RESOURCES

Unit Resources *Letters from Rifka*

BULLETIN BOARD IDEAS *Letters from Rifka*

1. Save one corner of the board for the best of students' *Letters from Rifka* writing assignments. You may want to use background maps of Eastern Europe, Russia, the Atlantic Ocean, and New York city to represent the setting of the novel.

2. Take one of the word search puzzles from the extra activities packet and with a marker copy it over in a large size on the bulletin board. Write the clue words to find to one side. Invite students prior to and after class to find the words and circle them on the bulletin board.

3. Have students find or draw pictures that they think resemble the people and scenery in the book.

4. Invite students to help make an interactive bulletin board quiz. Give each student a half-sheet of paper (about 4"x5') folded in half so that it can open. On the outside flap, have each student write a description of one of the characters in the text. On the inside, they will write the name of the character. You can staple or tack these papers to the bulletin board so that the students can read the descriptions and lift the flaps to find the answers.

5. Collect and display pictures of Russian cities from around 1919, Russian soldiers, peasants and Russian Jews, Antwerp, Warsaw, immigrant ships, the Statue of Liberty, and Ellis Island.

6. Display articles about the plight of the Russian Jews and their immigration to America during the early 1900s. Also display articles about the diseases mentioned in the novel: typhus and ringworm.

7. Display articles about the author, Karen Hesse.

8. Have students design postcards depicting the settings of the book.

9. Have students copy and illustrate the quotes from Pushkin that begin each chapter.

Unit Resources *Letters from Rifka*

EXTRA ACTIVITIES PACKET *Letters from Rifka*

One of the difficulties in teaching a novel is that all students don't read at the same speed. One student who likes to read may take the book home and finish it in a day or two. Sometimes a few students finish the in-class assignments early. The problem, then, is finding suitable extra activities for students.

One thing that helps is to keep a little library in the classroom. For this unit on *Letters from Rifka* you might check out from the school or public library other books (biographies, journals, autobiographies, etc.) about immigrant Russian Jews and other books set in that time frame. Information about careers in the field of immigration, teaching English as a second language, or information about being a host or foster family might be of interest to some students. Books compiling letters or journal entries from other people would be good to keep in your classroom. Some students may like reading letters rather than a regular novel format. It would be a good way to acquaint students with other people in history.

Your students who have reading difficulties, or speak English as a second language may benefit from listening to all or part of the book on tape. *Letters from Rifka* is available commercially, or you may want to have an adult or a student who reads well tape record the book for you.

Other things you may keep on hand are word search puzzles. Several puzzles relating directly to *Letters from Rifka* are included in the unit. Feel free to duplicate them. More puzzles, games and worksheets are available in the Puzzle Pack™ for *Letters From Rifka*, also available from Teacher's Pet Publications.

Some students may like to draw. You might devise a contest or allow some extra-credit grade for students who draw characters or scenes from *Letters from Rifka.* Note, too, that if the students do not want to keep their drawings you may pick up some extra bulletin board materials this way. If you have a contest and you supply the prize. You could, possibly, make the drawing itself a nonrefundable entry fee.

Have maps, a globe, and travel brochures on hand for easy reference. Travel agencies and automobile clubs are good sources for these materials.

The pages which follow contain games, puzzles, and worksheets. The keys, when appropriate, immediately follow the puzzle or worksheet. There are two main groups of activities: one group for the unit; that is, generally relating to the *Letters from Rifka* text, and another group of activities related strictly to the *Letters from Rifka* vocabulary.

Directions for the games, puzzles, and worksheets are self-explanatory. The object here is to provide you with extra materials you may use in any way you choose.

Unit Resources *Letters from Rifka*

MORE ACTIVITIES *Letters from Rifka*

1. Pick one of the incidents for students to dramatize. Encourage students to write dialog for the characters. (Perhaps you could assign various stories to different groups of students so more than one story could be acted and more students could participate.)

2. Have students design a bulletin board (ready to be put up; not just sketched) for *Letters from Rifka*.

3. Invite someone to talk to the class about the Russian Jews who immigrated to America.

4. Have someone from an aid society such as the Red Cross talk to the class about their work.

5. Ask the school nurse to explain how typhus and ringworm used to be treated around 1919 and how they are treated now.

6. Help students design and produce a talk show. Choose one of the story incidents as the topic. The host will interview the various characters. (Students should make up the questions they want the host to ask the characters.)

7. Have students work in pairs to create an interview with one of the characters. One student should be the interviewer and the other should be the interviewee. Students can work together to compose questions for the interviewer to ask. Each pair of students could present their interview to the class.

8. Invite students who have read other books by Karen Hesse to present booktalks to the class.

9. Invite students who have read other books on a similar topic as *Letters from Rifka* to present booktalks to the class.

10. Use some of the related topics (noted earlier for an in-class library) as topics for research, reports, or written papers, or as topics for guest speakers.

11. Invite someone who has lived in or visited one of the areas mentioned in the book to speak to the class.

12. Have students hold small group discussions related to topics in the book. Assign a recorder and a speaker for each group. Have the speaker from each group make a report to the class.

Unit Resources *Letters from Rifka*

MORE ACTIVITIES *Letters from Rifka*

13. Use the Internet to take a virtual field trip to the site of Ellis Island.

14. Research the life of Karen Hesse.

15. Research Russian history from the early 1900s.

16. If possible, speak with someone whose relatives or friends immigrated from Russia or another European country during the early 1900s.

17. Bring in Russian, Yiddish, and American music from the 1919-1920s era.

18. Write additional chapters for the book, telling what was happening in Russia from the time Rifka and her family left Berdichev until they settled in America.

19. Find out how and where immigrants are processed now when they arrive in the United States.

20. Find out more about the history of the Russian Jews during the Russian revolution.

21. Find out more about how the immigrants lived when they came to America.

22. Research the clothing of the era. Draw outfits, print them from web sites, or cut out pictures from old magazines. Create a bulletin board showing the clothing. Compare and contrast the clothes the immigrants wore in their home countries with those they wore in America.

23. Play language tapes in Yiddish, Russian, Flemish, and Polish. Help students learn a few words in each language.

24. Have students read more poems by Pushkin. They can read or recite a favorite poem and tell why they like it.

WORD SEARCH Letters From Rifka

```
G L Y Z N H M G D C B S U H P Y T R R W
B A L D E N I A R K U E V L E W T U V P
S V R K B B E S R Z H V R L N R S T O K
U L O W R R J T A I Y I R D O S R H R B
N L B G O X T O E A E F S I I R N I A A
C A R F T L C N B C C N A N C Z K N R
L W Q J A R G D N R L I N E K G H T G G
E F W I N L E N E E K H W P Z F W E E Y
K F C X I S R A V H N O H F R E V O V S
D O Z S F B M E S B B W A S R A W P R D
S U H H T A R U M U A P T P Q B Y O A M
V R Y Y I N P O C N R S A D Z T P E V M
R T J R Y A K K W D T E K C O L A M R N
N E S E K N S E Y N V C F I P Y P S U L
Y E S K K A D R B O A T I V N I E M M K
E N S A D I E C A L Y O R K n D R I C H
G L Y B U S T H B B I T M o R D E L O D
D L L T V L A I Q M D B r P Q I T K U Z
I R M I K T L E M O K a E H M S E M S M
V X I H S T O F P T A J H R U H I A I F
A S T A V O C V O Z T T Z V T S P N N V
D H Z N L V O V L I R G F R L Y B V Q V
V A V N D A H K I V I S C N A T H A N B
L W A A W H C G S G N I H T O L C N N S
N L H H H C F B H S A G I Z E L L E M D
```

ANTWERP	CLEVER	HUSBAND	ORANGE	SOCIAL
ASKIN	CLOTHING	ILYA	PAPER	TOVAH
AVRUM	COUSIN	ISAAC	PIETER	TREASURE
AARON	CREAM	KATRINA	POEMS	TWELVE
BABY	DAVID	KERCHIEF	POLISH	TYPHUS
BAKERY	ELLIS	LIBERTY	PRAYER	UKRAINE
BALD	ENGLISH	LOCKET	PUSHKIN	UNCLE
BANANA	FIVE	LOKEH	READ	WARSAW
BERDICHEV	FOURTEEN	MARIE	RIFKA	YIDDISH
BLACK	GASTON	MILKMAN	RINGWORM	YORK
BLOND	GIZELLE	MITZVAH	RUSSIAN	ZEB
BOWEN	HANNAH	MOTZIV	RUTH	
BROWN	HAT	NATHAN	SADIE	
CAR	HERRING	NEBROT	SAUL	
CHOCOLATE	HIAS	ONE	SHAWL	

WORD SEARCH ANSWER KEY Letters From Rifka

ANTWERP	CLEVER	HUSBAND	ORANGE	SOCIAL
ASKIN	CLOTHING	ILYA	PAPER	TOVAH
AVRUM	COUSIN	ISAAC	PIETER	TREASURE
AARON	CREAM	KATRINA	POEMS	TWELVE
BABY	DAVID	KERCHIEF	POLISH	TYPHUS
BAKERY	ELLIS	LIBERTY	PRAYER	UKRAINE
BALD	ENGLISH	LOCKET	PUSHKIN	UNCLE
BANANA	FIVE	LOKEH	READ	WARSAW
BERDICHEV	FOURTEEN	MARIE	RIFKA	YIDDISH
BLACK	GASTON	MILKMAN	RINGWORM	YORK
BLOND	GIZELLE	MITZVAH	RUSSIAN	ZEB
BOWEN	HANNAH	MOTZIV	RUTH	
BROWN	HAT	NATHAN	SADIE	
CAR	HERRING	NEBROT	SAUL	
CHOCOLATE	HIAS	ONE	SHAWL	

CROSSWORD Letters From Rifka

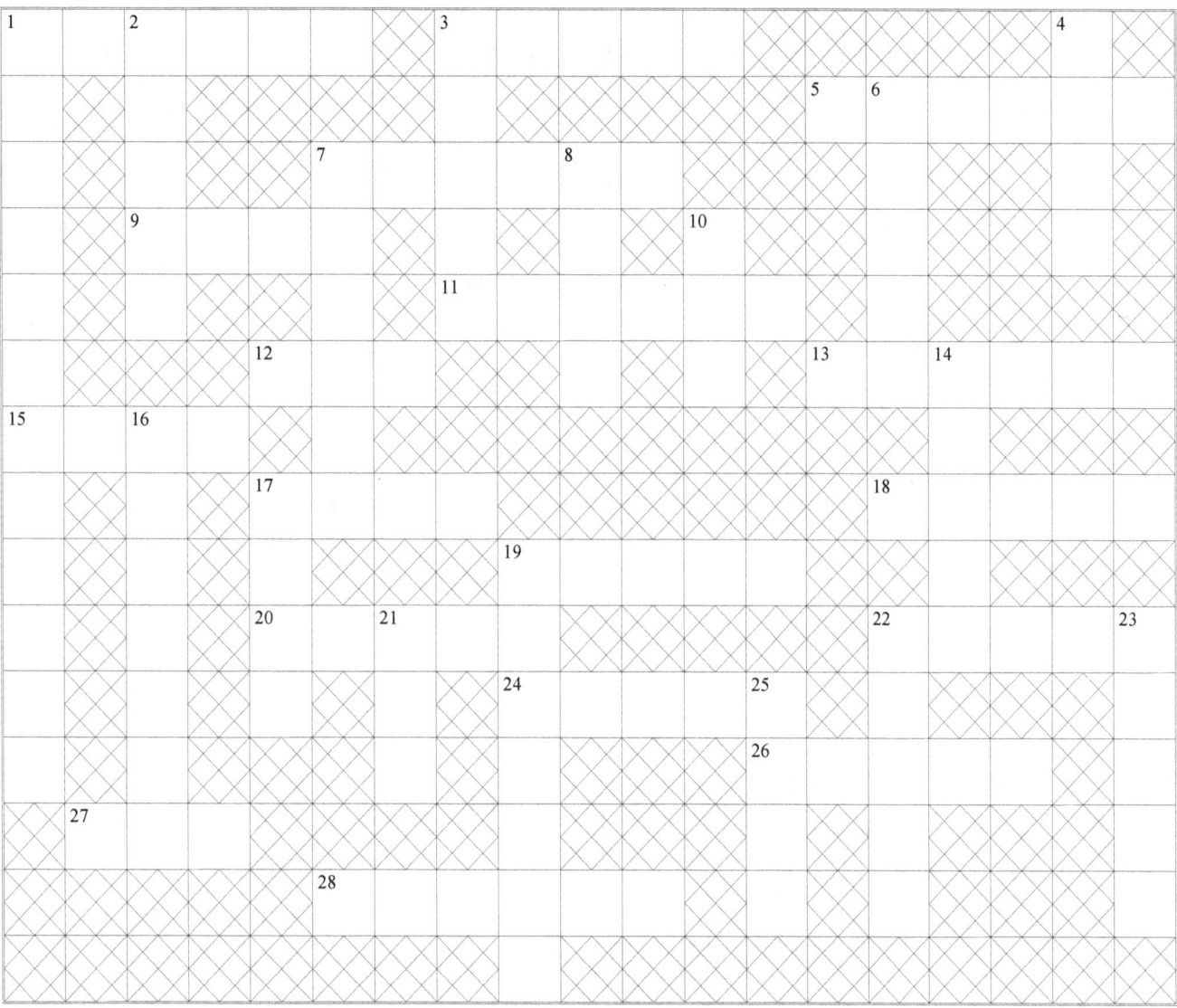

Across
1. Adjective describing Rifka: smartly resourceful
3. Helpful uncle
5. Rifka says it instead of scratching her head: Catholic ___
7. Nathan works in one
9. Russian peasant boy Rifka befriends
11. Brother who escapes from Russian army
12. Rifka buys one in Antwerp
13. Belgian man who takes care of Rifka
15. He is about to be drafted into the army.
17. Rifka's condition due to ringworm
18. Belgian woman who takes care of Rifka
19. Rifka's baby nephew
20. Hair color of the rest of the family
22. Rifka's hair color
24. Person to whom Rifka writes her letters
26. Rifka's brother who owns a car
27. Milkman reminded Rifka of this uncle
28. Family's last name

Down
1. They are stolen by Polish guards.
2. Island where Rifka must stay in the hospital
3. Doctor who helps Rifka learn English
4. Rifka teaches Ilya to do it
6. Russian Jewish immigrant girl who comes to America
7. Saul is surprised that Rifka knows what it is
8. Rifka's grandmother: Bubbe ___
10. Method of transportation home from hospital
14. Papa gives it to Rifka: prayer ___
16. Area of Russia where Rifka lived
17. Dies from typhus
19. City in Belgium where Rifka stays for treatment
21. Number of years Rifka was bald
22. Color of Rifka's velvet hat
23. Rifka makes one out of straw: Star of ___
25. Helps Jewish families with problems

CROSSWORD ANSWER KEY Letters From Rifka

¹C	L	²E	V	E	R		³A	V	R	U	M		⁴R
A		L			S					⁵P	⁶R	A	Y	E	R
N		L		⁷B	A	K	E	R	⁸Y		I		A
D		⁹I	L	Y	A		I		¹⁰U		C		F		D
L		S		N		¹¹N	A	T	H	A	N		K
E			¹²H	A	T		H		R		¹³G	¹⁴A	S	T	O	N
¹⁵S	¹⁶A	U	L		N							H
T		K		¹⁷B	A	L	D				¹⁸M	A	R	I	E
I		R		A		¹⁹A	a	r	o	n		W
C		A		²⁰B	²¹R	O	W	N			²²B	L	O	N	²³D
K		I		Y		N		²⁴T	O	V	²⁵A	H			A
S		N				E		W			²⁶I	S	A	A	C	V
	²⁷Z	E	B					E			A		C		I
				²⁸N	E	B	R	O	T		S		K		D
							P						

Across
1. Adjective describing Rifka: smartly resourceful
3. Helpful uncle
5. Rifka says it instead of scratching her head: Catholic ___
7. Nathan works in one
9. Russian peasant boy Rifka befriends
11. Brother who escapes from Russian army
12. Rifka buys one in Antwerp
13. Belgian man who takes care of Rifka
15. He is about to be drafted into the army.
17. Rifka's condition due to ringworm
18. Belgian woman who takes care of Rifka
19. Rifka's baby nephew
20. Hair color of the rest of the family
22. Rifka's hair color
24. Person to whom Rifka writes her letters
26. Rifka's brother who owns a car
27. Milkman reminded Rifka of this uncle
28. Family's last name

Down
1. They are stolen by Polish guards.
2. Island where Rifka must stay in the hospital
3. Doctor who helps Rifka learn English
4. Rifka teaches Ilya to do it
6. Russian Jewish immigrant girl who comes to America
7. Saul is surprised that Rifka knows what it is
8. Rifka's grandmother: Bubbe ____
10. Method of transportation home from hospital
14. Papa gives it to Rifka: prayer ___
16. Area of Russia where Rifka lived
17. Dies from typhus
19. City in Belgium where Rifka stays for treatment
21. Number of years Rifka was bald
22. Color of Rifka's velvet hat
23. Rifka makes one out of straw: Star of ___
25. Helps Jewish families with problems

MATCHING 1 Letters From Rifka

___ 1. COUSIN
___ 2. SAUL
___ 3. UKRAINE
___ 4. ANTWERP
___ 5. POLISH
___ 6. GIZELLE
___ 7. FARGATE
___ 8. CREAM
___ 9. YIDDISH
___ 10. READ
___ 11. ILYA
___ 12. FIVE
___ 13. ONE
___ 14. MOTZIV
___ 15. Aaron
___ 16. BLOND
___ 17. ORANGE
___ 18. UNCLE
___ 19. MARIE
___ 20. RUSSIAN
___ 21. KERCHIEF
___ 22. FOURTEEN
___ 23. CLOTHING
___ 24. BOWEN
___ 25. ISAAC

A. Gives Rifka a pack of paper and helps her learn English: Nurse ___
B. Mama and Papa work in one: ___ factory
C. Rifka's baby nephew
D. Belgian woman who takes care of Rifka
E. Rifka's hair color
F. Rifka wears one over her bald head
G. Number of brothers Rifka has
H. He is about to be drafted into the army.
I. Polish city where family stayed during typhus illness
J. Tovah's relationship to Rifka
K. Rifka speaks it without an accent
L. City in Belgium where Rifka stays for treatment
M. Russian peasant boy Rifka befriends
N. Rifka's older brothers left this many years ago
O. Area of Russia where Rifka lived
P. Street seller takes all of Rifka's money for one
Q. Ilya's relative in America
R. Number of years Rifka was bald
S. Rifka learns this language in Motziv
T. Rifka gets it in Antwerp from a man with a cart: ice ___
U. Rifka teaches Ilya to do it
V. Allows Rifka to enter America: Mr. ___
W. Rifka's brother who owns a car
X. One of Rifka's playmates in Antwerp
Y. Rifka's native language

MATCHING 1 ANSWER KEY Letters From Rifka

J - 1. COUSIN	A.	Gives Rifka a pack of paper and helps her learn English: Nurse ___
H - 2. SAUL	B.	Mama and Papa work in one: ___ factory
O - 3. UKRAINE	C.	Rifka's baby nephew
L - 4. ANTWERP	D.	Belgian woman who takes care of Rifka
S - 5. POLISH	E.	Rifka's hair color
X - 6. GIZELLE	F.	Rifka wears one over her bald head
V - 7. FARGATE	G.	Number of brothers Rifka has
T - 8. CREAM	H.	He is about to be drafted into the army.
Y - 9. YIDDISH	I.	Polish city where family stayed during typhus illness
U -10. READ	J.	Tovah's relationship to Rifka
M -11. ILYA	K.	Rifka speaks it without an accent
G -12. FIVE	L.	City in Belgium where Rifka stays for treatment
R -13. ONE	M.	Russian peasant boy Rifka befriends
I -14. MOTZIV	N.	Rifka's older brothers left this many years ago
C -15. Aaron	O.	Area of Russia where Rifka lived
E -16. BLOND	P.	Street seller takes all of Rifka's money for one
P -17. ORANGE	Q.	Ilya's relative in America
Q -18. UNCLE	R.	Number of years Rifka was bald
D -19. MARIE	S.	Rifka learns this language in Motziv
K -20. RUSSIAN	T.	Rifka gets it in Antwerp from a man with a cart: ice ___
F -21. KERCHIEF	U.	Rifka teaches Ilya to do it
N -22. FOURTEEN	V.	Allows Rifka to enter America: Mr. ___
B -23. CLOTHING	W.	Rifka's brother who owns a car
A -24. BOWEN	X.	One of Rifka's playmates in Antwerp
W 25. ISAAC	Y.	Rifka's native language

MATCHING 2 Letters From Rifka

___ 1. POEMS　　　　　　　A. Took piano lessons

___ 2. BOWEN　　　　　　　B. Rifka's hair color

___ 3. BLOND　　　　　　　C. Rifka says it instead of scratching her head: Catholic ___

___ 4. CREAM　　　　　　　D. Rifka writes her own

___ 5. BABY　　　　　　　　E. Rifka's uncle's horse

___ 6. POLISH　　　　　　　F. Rifka's condition due to ringworm

___ 7. RIFKA　　　　　　　G. Young sailor Rifka meets on the ship

___ 8. HANNAH　　　　　　H. Russian peasant boy Rifka befriends

___ 9. KERCHIEF　　　　　I. One of Rifka's playmates in Antwerp

___10. BROWN　　　　　　J. Russian Jewish immigrant girl who comes to America

___11. CHOCOLATE　　　　K. Rifka makes one out of straw: Star of ___

___12. ZEB　　　　　　　　L. They are stolen by Polish guards.

___13. PRAYER　　　　　　M. Rifka wears one over her bald head

___14. DAVID　　　　　　　N. Rifka gets it in Antwerp from a man with a cart: ice ___

___15. ILYA　　　　　　　　O. Rifka buys one in Antwerp

___16. PIETER　　　　　　P. Milkman reminded Rifka of this uncle

___17. GIZELLE　　　　　　Q. Family's home city in Ukraine

___18. LOKEH　　　　　　　R. Dies from typhus

___19. CANDLESTICKS　　S. Polish city where family stayed during typhus illness

___20. BALD　　　　　　　　T. Language Rifka learns in Antwerp

___21. NEBROT　　　　　　U. Rifka learns this language in Motziv

___22. FLEMISH　　　　　　V. Rifka describes it as biting off a corner of heaven.

___23. MOTZIV　　　　　　W. Gives Rifka a pack of paper and helps her learn English: Nurse ___

___24. BERDICHEV　　　　X. Hair color of the rest of the family

___25. HAT　　　　　　　　Y. Family's last name

MATCHING 2 ANSWER KEY Letters From Rifka

D - 1.	POEMS	A. Took piano lessons
W - 2.	BOWEN	B. Rifka's hair color
B - 3.	BLOND	C. Rifka says it instead of scratching her head: Catholic ___
N - 4.	CREAM	D. Rifka writes her own
R - 5.	BABY	E. Rifka's uncle's horse
U - 6.	POLISH	F. Rifka's condition due to ringworm
J - 7.	RIFKA	G. Young sailor Rifka meets on the ship
A - 8.	HANNAH	H. Russian peasant boy Rifka befriends
M - 9.	KERCHIEF	I. One of Rifka's playmates in Antwerp
X -10.	BROWN	J. Russian Jewish immigrant girl who comes to America
V -11.	CHOCOLATE	K. Rifka makes one out of straw: Star of ___
P -12.	ZEB	L. They are stolen by Polish guards.
C -13.	PRAYER	M. Rifka wears one over her bald head
K -14.	DAVID	N. Rifka gets it in Antwerp from a man with a cart: ice ___
H -15.	ILYA	O. Rifka buys one in Antwerp
G -16.	PIETER	P. Milkman reminded Rifka of this uncle
I - 17.	GIZELLE	Q. Family's home city in Ukraine
E -18.	LOKEH	R. Dies from typhus
L -19.	CANDLESTICKS	S. Polish city where family stayed during typhus illness
F -20.	BALD	T. Language Rifka learns in Antwerp
Y -21.	NEBROT	U. Rifka learns this language in Motziv
T -22.	FLEMISH	V. Rifka describes it as biting off a corner of heaven.
S -23.	MOTZIV	W. Gives Rifka a pack of paper and helps her learn English: Nurse ___
Q -24.	BERDICHEV	X. Hair color of the rest of the family
O -25.	HAT	Y. Family's last name

JUGGLE LETTERS 1 Letters From Rifka

1. DLBA = 1. _____
   Rifka's condition due to ringworm

2. IAHS = 2. _____
   Helps Jewish families with problems

3. INOSUC = 3. _____
   Tovah's relationship to Rifka

4. INHLGCOT = 4. _____
   Mama and Papa work in one: ___ factory

5. CELUN = 5. _____
   Ilya's relative in America

6. IATNARK = 6. _____
   Sister who treats Rifka's ringworm & gives her chocolate

7. FRIAK = 7. _____
   Russian Jewish immigrant girl who comes to America

8. BVIHCRDEE = 8. _____
   Family's home city in Ukraine

9. CHKEFERI = 9. _____
   Rifka wears one over her bald head

10. AULS =10. _____
    He is about to be drafted into the army.

11. PEAWTNR =11. _____
    City in Belgium where Rifka stays for treatment

12. SSNKIDTELCAC =12. _____
    They are stolen by Polish guards.

13. PHTSYU =13. _____
    Rifka gets this disease when entering Poland.

14. EGAFRAT =14. _____
    Allows Rifka to enter America: Mr. ___

15. NUSAISR =15. _____
    Rifka speaks it without an accent

JUGGLE LETTERS 1 ANSWER KEY Letters From Rifka

1. DLBA = 1. BALD
Rifka's condition due to ringworm

2. IAHS = 2. HIAS
Helps Jewish families with problems

3. INOSUC = 3. COUSIN
Tovah's relationship to Rifka

4. INHLGCOT = 4. CLOTHING
Mama and Papa work in one: ___ factory

5. CELUN = 5. UNCLE
Ilya's relative in America

6. IATNARK = 6. KATRINA
Sister who treats Rifka's ringworm & gives her chocolate

7. FRIAK = 7. RIFKA
Russian Jewish immigrant girl who comes to America

8. BVIHCRDEE = 8. BERDICHEV
Family's home city in Ukraine

9. CHKEFERI = 9. KERCHIEF
Rifka wears one over her bald head

10. AULS =10. SAUL
He is about to be drafted into the army.

11. PEAWTNR =11. ANTWERP
City in Belgium where Rifka stays for treatment

12. SSNKIDTELCAC =12. CANDLESTICKS
They are stolen by Polish guards.

13. PHTSYU =13. TYPHUS
Rifka gets this disease when entering Poland.

14. EGAFRAT =14. FARGATE
Allows Rifka to enter America: Mr. ___

15. NUSAISR =15. RUSSIAN
Rifka speaks it without an accent

JUGGLE LETTERS 1 Letters From Rifka

1. LIOASC   = 1. _____
                    American government fears Rifka will become a ___ responsibility.

2. TRSEUERA   = 2. _____
                    Pieter tells Rifka she is one to her family

3. WBEON   = 3. _____
                    Gives Rifka a pack of paper and helps her learn English: Nurse ___

4. ORMRGWIN   = 4. _____
                    Rifka gets it from a peasant girl

5. RAPYER   = 5. _____
                    Rifka says it instead of scratching her head: Catholic ___

6. OLDBN   = 6. _____
                    Rifka's hair color

7. IZATVHM   = 7. _____
                    Rifka has one for her birthday

8. ASSKNLDIECTC   = 8. _____
                    They are stolen by Polish guards.

9. UHRT   = 9. _____
                    Rifka's grandmother: Bubbe ____

10. ERAGTFA   =10. _____
                    Allows Rifka to enter America: Mr. ___

11. PRAEP   =11. _____
                    Rifka asks Nurse Bowen for it

12. ERFICHEK   =12. _____
                    Rifka wears one over her bald head

13. CDERBIVHE   =13. _____
                    Family's home city in Ukraine

14. EIFV   =14. _____
                    Number of brothers Rifka has

15. GCNOHLTI   =15. _____
                    Mama and Papa work in one: ___ factory

JUGGLE LETTERS 2 ANSWER KEY Letters From Rifka

1. LIOASC = 1. SOCIAL
American government fears Rifka will become a ___ responsibility.

2. TRSEUERA = 2. TREASURE
Pieter tells Rifka she is one to her family

3. WBEON = 3. BOWEN
Gives Rifka a pack of paper and helps her learn English: Nurse ___

4. ORMRGWIN = 4. RINGWORM
Rifka gets it from a peasant girl

5. RAPYER = 5. PRAYER
Rifka says it instead of scratching her head: Catholic ___

6. OLDBN = 6. BLOND
Rifka's hair color

7. IZATVHM = 7. MITZVAH
Rifka has one for her birthday

8. ASSKNLDIECTC = 8. CANDLESTICKS
They are stolen by Polish guards.

9. UHRT = 9. RUTH
Rifka's grandmother: Bubbe ___

10. ERAGTFA = 10. FARGATE
Allows Rifka to enter America: Mr. ___

11. PRAEP = 11. PAPER
Rifka asks Nurse Bowen for it

12. ERFICHEK = 12. KERCHIEF
Rifka wears one over her bald head

13. CDERBIVHE = 13. BERDICHEV
Family's home city in Ukraine

14. EIFV = 14. FIVE
Number of brothers Rifka has

15. GCNOHLTI = 15. CLOTHING
Mama and Papa work in one: ___ factory

Letters From Rifka Word List

No.	Word	Clue/Definition
1.	ANTWERP	City in Belgium where Rifka stays for treatment
2.	ASKIN	Doctor who helps Rifka learn English
3.	AVRUM	Helpful uncle
4.	Aaron	Rifka's baby nephew
5.	BABY	Dies from typhus
6.	BAKERY	Nathan works in one
7.	BALD	Rifka's condition due to ringworm
8.	BANANA	Saul is surprised that Rifka knows what it is
9.	BERDICHEV	Family's home city in Ukraine
10.	BLACK	Color of Rifka's velvet hat
11.	BLOND	Rifka's hair color
12.	BOWEN	Gives Rifka a pack of paper and helps her learn English: Nurse ___
13.	BROWN	Hair color of the rest of the family
14.	CANDLESTICKS	They are stolen by Polish guards.
15.	CAR	Method of transportation home from hospital
16.	CHOCOLATE	Rifka describes it as biting off a corner of heaven.
17.	CLEVER	Adjective describing Rifka: smartly resourceful
18.	CLOTHING	Mama and Papa work in one: ___ factory
19.	COUSIN	Tovah's relationship to Rifka
20.	CREAM	Rifka gets it in Antwerp from a man with a cart: ice ___
21.	DAVID	Rifka makes one out of straw: Star of ___
22.	ELLIS	Island where Rifka must stay in the hospital
23.	ENGLISH	Rifka learns this language in the hospital
24.	FARGATE	Allows Rifka to enter America: Mr. ___
25.	FIVE	Number of brothers Rifka has
26.	FLEMISH	Language Rifka learns in Antwerp
27.	FOURTEEN	Rifka's older brothers left this many years ago
28.	GASTON	Belgian man who takes care of Rifka
29.	GIZELLE	One of Rifka's playmates in Antwerp
30.	HANNAH	Took piano lessons
31.	HAT	Rifka buys one in Antwerp
32.	HERRING	Innkeeper's daughter steals it and a roll
33.	HIAS	Helps Jewish families with problems
34.	HUSBAND	Rifka fears she will never get one
35.	ILYA	Russian peasant boy Rifka befriends
36.	ISAAC	Rifka's brother who owns a car
37.	KATRINA	Sister who treats Rifka's ringworm & gives her chocolate
38.	KERCHIEF	Rifka wears one over her bald head
39.	LIBERTY	Rifka sees it in New York Harbor: Statue of ___
40.	LOCKET	Mama gives it to Rifka: gold ___
41.	LOKEH	Rifka's uncle's horse
42.	MARIE	Belgian woman who takes care of Rifka
43.	MILKMAN	Helps Rifka find her way home in Antwerp
44.	MITZVAH	Rifka has one for her birthday
45.	MOTZIV	Polish city where family stayed during typhus illness
46.	NATHAN	Brother who escapes from Russian army
47.	NEBROT	Family's last name
48.	ONE	Number of years Rifka was bald
49.	ORANGE	Street seller takes all of Rifka's money for one
50.	PAPER	Rifka asks Nurse Bowen for it
		Young sailor Rifka meets on the ship

Letters From Rifka Word List

51. PIETER — Young sailor Rifka meets on the ship
52. POEMS — Rifka writes her own
53. POLISH — Rifka learns this language in Motziv
54. PRAYER — Rifka says it instead of scratching her head: Catholic ___
55. PUSHKIN — Russian author of Rifka's poetry book
56. READ — Rifka teaches Ilya to do it
57. RIFKA — Russian Jewish immigrant girl who comes to America
58. RINGWORM — Rifka gets it from a peasant girl
59. RUSSIAN — Rifka speaks it without an accent
60. RUTH — Rifka's grandmother: Bubbe ___
61. SADIE — Chenowitz girl from Berdichev who married Rifka's brother
62. SAUL — He is about to be drafted into the army.
63. SHAWL — Papa gives it to Rifka: prayer ___
64. SIMPLETON — Mr. Fargate believed this of Ilya
65. SOCIAL — American government fears Rifka will become a ___ responsibility.
66. TOVAH — Person to whom Rifka writes her letters
67. TREASURE — Pieter tells Rifka she is one to her family
68. TWELVE — Rifka's age when she leaves Russia
69. TYPHUS — Rifka gets this disease when entering Poland.
70. UKRAINE — Area of Russia where Rifka lived
71. UNCLE — Ilya's relative in America
72. WARSAW — Family gets the steamship to America in this city
73. YIDDISH — Rifka's native language
74. YORK — Family moves to this American city: New ___
75. ZEB — Milkman reminded Rifka of this uncle

VOCABULARY RESOURCE MATERIALS

VOCABULARY WORD SEARCH Letters From Rifka

```
I P F J S U O I G A T N O C S O M F H P
Y M R S D T Z V M C O H R O P D I R U B
I T M O C L A S P I N G P M R D S A D X
M N D I W C C M T M J L H M O A C G D F
V E T L G L P A M I L C A I U D H I L V
Z I B E W R G C D E L G N T T V I L E V
G N X R N I A E R Y R T C T L A E E D R
M E B G M T T N O M M I E E U N F L F T
T V D U Z N I T T L I H N D X T Y Z E S
D N F H E E Y O I H N C D G U A M M R P
N O G M G R R N N T I N E Q R G P U E T
R C R N X L U C O S M E H G Y E L V V Q
L O U N L W F C M E A T C B S B T B E M
T O X C M O C R K L L S U T Z X J J L C
L P S F H L C N F S Y Q O S W Y F V C Y
M L G K C C R K F U A R R L C N R D T S
N X X R I O P R E O C C C W I E T C H Q
B S Z G B P V W I T S J K Z R D A C H E
F W K B Y S P F S Y X S S S E R T S I D
Z O U K O F F E N S E S F L T S G K Y G
G T N U M B D N D R A W I S S H A W L F
S S F S H O Y Z V V C C I P L S F L J Y
F C O M M O T I O N A D E G N U L P O S
F R E N Z I E D H T P R E C I O U S Z N
G N O I T U A C E R P M A R G I N S M K
```

ACHE	DENY	LOUNGE	PLUNGED	STENCH
ADVANTAGE	DISTRACT	LUXURY	PRECAUTION	STOW
BLUR	DISTRESS	MARGINS	PRECIOUS	STUBBORN
CLASPING	FRAGILE	MINIMAL	PROWL	TEMPEST
CLEVER	FRENZIED	MISCHIEF	RUCKSACK	TILTED
COMMITTED	FUMIGATION	MODEST	SALON	TORMENTED
COMMOTION	FURY	MONITOR	SHAWL	TOUSLE
CONTAGIOUS	HUDDLED	NUMB	SKIPPED	WARD
CONVENIENT	IMMIGRANT	ODD	SOLID	WITS
CROUCHED	INTENTIONS	OFFENSES	SPROUT	
DELICATE	LOCKET	ORPHAN	STAMMERING	

VOCABULARY WORD SEARCH ANSWER KEY Letters From Rifka

ACHE	DENY	LOUNGE	PLUNGED	STENCH
ADVANTAGE	DISTRACT	LUXURY	PRECAUTION	STOW
BLUR	DISTRESS	MARGINS	PRECIOUS	STUBBORN
CLASPING	FRAGILE	MINIMAL	PROWL	TEMPEST
CLEVER	FRENZIED	MISCHIEF	RUCKSACK	TILTED
COMMITTED	FUMIGATION	MODEST	SALON	TORMENTED
COMMOTION	FURY	MONITOR	SHAWL	TOUSLE
CONTAGIOUS	HUDDLED	NUMB	SKIPPED	WARD
CONVENIENT	IMMIGRANT	ODD	SOLID	WITS
CROUCHED	INTENTIONS	OFFENSES	SPROUT	
DELICATE	LOCKET	ORPHAN	STAMMERING	

VOCABULARY CROSSWORD Letters From Rifka

Across
1. Humble; not showing off
3. Intelligence; common sense
5. Backpack
7. Spread from one person to another
11. Become fuzzy or unclear
12. A treatment for getting rid of bugs or disease
13. Disagree; say something is not true
15. Blank spaces around the print on a page
18. Harmless misbehavior; naughtiness
21. Anger
23. Strong; firm
24. Move around in a sneaky way
25. Child whose parents are dead
26. Unusual; strange

Down
2. Pale, gentle, and soft
4. Piece of fabric worn over the shoulders
6. Smart; intelligent; resourceful
8. Severe storm with strong winds and rain
9. Put something away for future use
10. Plans; purposes
12. Quickly and with excitement
13. Suffering; discomfort
14. Not able to feel sensations
16. To want something very much
17. Grow quickly
19. Willful; not cooperative
20. Full of uncontrolled anger or excitement
22. Elegant room in a private home

VOCABULARY CROSSWORD ANSWER KEY Letters From Rifka

			¹M	O	²D	E	S	T		³W	I	T	⁴S	
					E								H	
					L			⁵R	⁶U	C	K	S	A	C	K
	⁷C	O	⁸T	A	G	I	O	U	S		L		W	
¹⁰I			E				C		T		E		¹¹B	L	U	R
N	¹²F	U	M	I	G	A	T	I	O	N		V		
T	R		P			T			W			E		
E	A		E		¹³D	E	¹⁴N	Y	¹⁵M	¹⁶A	R	G	I	N	¹⁷S
N	N		S		I		U			C					P
T	T		T		S		¹⁸M	I	¹⁹S	C	H	I	²⁰E	F		R
I	I				T		B		T				F			O
O	C		²¹F	U	R	Y			U				F			U
N	A				E				B		²²S		E			T
²³S	O	L	I	D					B		A		R			
			L		S		²⁴P	R	O	W	L		V			
			Y						R		O		E			
				²⁵O	R	P	H	A	N		²⁶N	O	D	D

Across
1. Humble; not showing off
3. Intelligence; common sense
5. Backpack
7. Spread from one person to another
11. Become fuzzy or unclear
12. A treatment for getting rid of bugs or disease
13. Disagree; say something is not true
15. Blank spaces around the print on a page
18. Harmless misbehavior; naughtiness
21. Anger
23. Strong; firm
24. Move around in a sneaky way
25. Child whose parents are dead
26. Unusual; strange

Down
2. Pale, gentle, and soft
4. Piece of fabric worn over the shoulders
6. Smart; intelligent; resourceful
8. Severe storm with strong winds and rain
9. Put something away for future use
10. Plans; purposes
12. Quickly and with excitement
13. Suffering; discomfort
14. Not able to feel sensations
16. To want something very much
17. Grow quickly
19. Willful; not cooperative
20. Full of uncontrolled anger or excitement
22. Elegant room in a private home

VOCABULARY MATCHING 1 Letters From Rifka

___ 1. WARD   A. Piece of fabric worn over the shoulders
___ 2. COMMOTION   B. Move around in a sneaky way
___ 3. ORPHAN   C. A favorable position
___ 4. BILLOWING   D. Watch over; check on
___ 5. DENY   E. Disagree; say something is not true
___ 6. FRANTICALLY   F. Hospital room for several patients
___ 7. CLEVER   G. Pale, gentle, and soft
___ 8. IMMIGRANT   H. Suffering; discomfort
___ 9. SALON   I. Inflicted pain or discomfort
___10. DEPORTATION   J. Smart; intelligent; resourceful
___11. TILTED   K. Removal of a foreigner from a country
___12. MODEST   L. Slanted; leaning at an angle
___13. SHAWL   M. A public room for relaxing
___14. COMMITTED   N. Elegant room in a private home
___15. LOUNGE   O. Rolling or flowing upward
___16. PROWL   P. Not strong; easily broken
___17. WITS   Q. Noisy activity
___18. SOLID   R. Quickly and with excitement
___19. ADVANTAGE   S. Intelligence; common sense
___20. MONITOR   T. Did something wrong
___21. DISTRESS   U. Child whose parents are dead
___22. TORMENTED   V. Humble; not showing off
___23. TOUSLE   W. Tangle or mess up hair
___24. DELICATE   X. Someone who settles in a country other than their native one
___25. FRAGILE   Y. Strong; firm

VOCABULARY MATCHING 1 ANSWER KEY Letters From Rifka

F - 1. WARD A. Piece of fabric worn over the shoulders
Q - 2. COMMOTION B. Move around in a sneaky way
U - 3. ORPHAN C. A favorable position
O - 4. BILLOWING D. Watch over; check on
E - 5. DENY E. Disagree; say something is not true
R - 6. FRANTICALLY F. Hospital room for several patients
J - 7. CLEVER G. Pale, gentle, and soft
X - 8. IMMIGRANT H. Suffering; discomfort
N - 9. SALON I. Inflicted pain or discomfort
K -10. DEPORTATION J. Smart; intelligent; resourceful
L -11. TILTED K. Removal of a foreigner from a country
V -12. MODEST L. Slanted; leaning at an angle
A -13. SHAWL M. A public room for relaxing
T -14. COMMITTED N. Elegant room in a private home
M -15. LOUNGE O. Rolling or flowing upward
B -16. PROWL P. Not strong; easily broken
S -17. WITS Q. Noisy activity
Y -18. SOLID R. Quickly and with excitement
C -19. ADVANTAGE S. Intelligence; common sense
D -20. MONITOR T. Did something wrong
H -21. DISTRESS U. Child whose parents are dead
I -22. TORMENTED V. Humble; not showing off
W 23. TOUSLE W. Tangle or mess up hair
G -24. DELICATE X. Someone who settles in a country other than their native one
P -25. FRAGILE Y. Strong; firm

VOCABULARY MATCHING 2 Letters From Rifka

___ 1. TILTED   A. Sections of a piece of writing

___ 2. DEPORTATION   B. Pale, gentle, and soft

___ 3. CLASPING   C. Put something away for future use

___ 4. DELICATE   D. Disagree; say something is not true

___ 5. MONITOR   E. Suffering; discomfort

___ 6. PASSAGES   F. Strong; firm

___ 7. WARD   G. A treatment for getting rid of bugs or disease

___ 8. DISTRESS   H. Full of uncontrolled anger or excitement

___ 9. DENY   I. Intelligence; common sense

___10. RUCKSACK   J. Did something wrong

___11. IMMIGRANT   K. Hospital room for several patients

___12. STOW   L. Blank spaces around the print on a page

___13. WITS   M. Speaking with many pauses and repetitions

___14. SPROUT   N. Anger

___15. ORPHAN   O. Grow quickly

___16. FURY   P. Removal of a foreigner from a country

___17. MARGINS   Q. A public room for relaxing

___18. MISCHIEF   R. Holding tightly

___19. FUMIGATION   S. Humble; not showing off

___20. LOUNGE   T. Slanted; leaning at an angle

___21. FRENZIED   U. Watch over; check on

___22. SOLID   V. Someone who settles in a country other than their native one

___23. STAMMERING   W. Backpack

___24. COMMITTED   X. Harmless misbehavior; naughtiness

___25. MODEST   Y. Child whose parents are dead

VOCABULARY MATCHING 2 ANSWER KEY Letters From Rifka

T - 1. TILTED	A.	Sections of a piece of writing
P - 2. DEPORTATION	B.	Pale, gentle, and soft
R - 3. CLASPING	C.	Put something away for future use
B - 4. DELICATE	D.	Disagree; say something is not true
U - 5. MONITOR	E.	Suffering; discomfort
A - 6. PASSAGES	F.	Strong; firm
K - 7. WARD	G.	A treatment for getting rid of bugs or disease
E - 8. DISTRESS	H.	Full of uncontrolled anger or excitement
D - 9. DENY	I.	Intelligence; common sense
W 10. RUCKSACK	J.	Did something wrong
V -11. IMMIGRANT	K.	Hospital room for several patients
C -12. STOW	L.	Blank spaces around the print on a page
I - 13. WITS	M.	Speaking with many pauses and repetitions
O -14. SPROUT	N.	Anger
Y -15. ORPHAN	O.	Grow quickly
N -16. FURY	P.	Removal of a foreigner from a country
L -17. MARGINS	Q.	A public room for relaxing
X -18. MISCHIEF	R.	Holding tightly
G -19. FUMIGATION	S.	Humble; not showing off
Q -20. LOUNGE	T.	Slanted; leaning at an angle
H -21. FRENZIED	U.	Watch over; check on
F -22. SOLID	V.	Someone who settles in a country other than their native one
M 23. STAMMERING	W.	Backpack
J - 24. COMMITTED	X.	Harmless misbehavior; naughtiness
S -25. MODEST	Y.	Child whose parents are dead

JUGGLE LETTERS 1 Letters From Rifka

1. RDEFEZIN = 1. _____
   Full of uncontrolled anger or excitement

2. OMMCDTIET = 2. _____
   Did something wrong

3. SAINGRM = 3. _____
   Blank spaces around the print on a page

4. MACNPOSOIS = 4. _____
   Kindness; consideration

5. NTOEINNCVE = 5. _____
   Useful; helpful; easy

6. AROHPN = 6. _____
   Child whose parents are dead

7. MTIONOMCO = 7. _____
   Noisy activity

8. WAHSL = 8. _____
   Piece of fabric worn over the shoulders

9. ADWR = 9. _____
   Hospital room for several patients

10. PPKEDIS = 10. _____
    Chose to not go to an activity

11. RUTOSP = 11. _____
    Grow quickly

12. CTKEOL = 12. _____
    Small metal case that holds a picture, often kept on a necklace

13. OPARINCTUE = 13. _____
    Action taken to protect against harm

14. WROLP = 14. _____
    Move around in a sneaky way

15. TCHSNE = 15. _____
    Foul, disgusting smell

JUGGLE LETTERS 1 ANSWER KEY Letters From Rifka

1. RDEFEZIN = 1. FRENZIED
Full of uncontrolled anger or excitement

2. OMMCDTIET = 2. COMMITTED
Did something wrong

3. SAINGRM = 3. MARGINS
Blank spaces around the print on a page

4. MACNPOSOIS = 4. COMPASSION
Kindness; consideration

5. NTOEINNCVE = 5. CONVENIENT
Useful; helpful; easy

6. AROHPN = 6. ORPHAN
Child whose parents are dead

7. MTIONOMCO = 7. COMMOTION
Noisy activity

8. WAHSL = 8. SHAWL
Piece of fabric worn over the shoulders

9. ADWR = 9. WARD
Hospital room for several patients

10. PPKEDIS =10. SKIPPED
Chose to not go to an activity

11. RUTOSP =11. SPROUT
Grow quickly

12. CTKEOL =12. LOCKET
Small metal case that holds a picture, often kept on a necklace

13. OPARINCTUE =13. PRECAUTION
Action taken to protect against harm

14. WROLP =14. PROWL
Move around in a sneaky way

15. TCHSNE =15. STENCH
Foul, disgusting smell

VOCABULARY JUGGLE 2 Letters From Rifka

1. ERTETDNMO = 1. _____
   Inflicted pain or discomfort

2. EVLREC = 2. _____
   Smart; intelligent; resourceful

3. TAONOPIRETD = 3. _____
   Removal of a foreigner from a country

4. CHEA = 4. _____
   To want something very much

5. EISTDSRS = 5. _____
   Suffering; discomfort

6. IZRNEDFE = 6. _____
   Full of uncontrolled anger or excitement

7. OSETLU = 7. _____
   Tangle or mess up hair

8. EOCHRUDC = 8. _____
   Bent close to the ground

9. TNOSUBBR = 9. _____
   Willful; not cooperative

10. URSTPO =10. _____
    Grow quickly

11. CSIADTTR =11. _____
    Take attention away from

12. LUNDPGE =12. _____
    Pushed firmly into a container

13. MITAFUNGOI =13. _____
    A treatment for getting rid of bugs or disease

14. OCGNOAIUST =14. _____
    Spread from one person to another

15. SSPAESGA =15. _____
    Sections of a piece of writing

VOCABULARY JUGGLE LETTERS 2 ANSWER KEY Letters From Rifka

1. ERTETDNMO = 1. TORMENTED
   Inflicted pain or discomfort

2. EVLREC = 2. CLEVER
   Smart; intelligent; resourceful

3. TAONOPIRETD = 3. DEPORTATION
   Removal of a foreigner from a country

4. CHEA = 4. ACHE
   To want something very much

5. EISTDSRS = 5. DISTRESS
   Suffering; discomfort

6. IZRNEDFE = 6. FRENZIED
   Full of uncontrolled anger or excitement

7. OSETLU = 7. TOUSLE
   Tangle or mess up hair

8. EOCHRUDC = 8. CROUCHED
   Bent close to the ground

9. TNOSUBBR = 9. STUBBORN
   Willful; not cooperative

10. URSTPO =10. SPROUT
    Grow quickly

11. CSIADTTR =11. DISTRACT
    Take attention away from

12. LUNDPGE =12. PLUNGED
    Pushed firmly into a container

13. MITAFUNGOI =13. FUMIGATION
    A treatment for getting rid of bugs or disease

14. OCGNOAIUST =14. CONTAGIOUS
    Spread from one person to another

15. SSPAESGA =15. PASSAGES
    Sections of a piece of writing

Letters From Rifka Vocabulary Word List

No.	Word	Clue/Definition
1.	ACHE	To want something very much
2.	ADVANTAGE	A favorable position
3.	BILLOWING	Rolling or flowing upward
4.	BLUR	Become fuzzy or unclear
5.	CLASPING	Holding tightly
6.	CLEVER	Smart; intelligent; resourceful
7.	COMMITTED	Did something wrong
8.	COMMOTION	Noisy activity
9.	COMPASSION	Kindness; consideration
10.	CONTAGIOUS	Spread from one person to another
11.	CONVENIENT	Useful; helpful; easy
12.	CROUCHED	Bent close to the ground
13.	DELICATE	Pale, gentle, and soft
14.	DENY	Disagree; say something is not true
15.	DEPORTATION	Removal of a foreigner from a country
16.	DISTRACT	Take attention away from
17.	DISTRESS	Suffering; discomfort
18.	FRAGILE	Not strong; easily broken
19.	FRANTICALLY	Quickly and with excitement
20.	FRENZIED	Full of uncontrolled anger or excitement
21.	FUMIGATION	A treatment for getting rid of bugs or disease
22.	FURY	Anger
23.	HUDDLED	Gathered together in a tight group
24.	IMMIGRANT	Someone who settles in a country other than their native one
25.	INTENTIONS	Plans; purposes
26.	LOCKET	Small metal case that holds a picture, often kept on a necklace
27.	LOUNGE	A public room for relaxing
28.	LUXURY	Expensive, high-quality comfort
29.	MARGINS	Blank spaces around the print on a page
30.	MINIMAL	A very small amount
31.	MISCHIEF	Harmless misbehavior; naughtiness
32.	MODEST	Humble; not showing off
33.	MONITOR	Watch over; check on
34.	NUMB	Not able to feel sensations
35.	ODD	Unusual; strange
36.	OFFENSES	Wrongdoings against usual standards
37.	ORPHAN	Child whose parents are dead
38.	PASSAGES	Sections of a piece of writing
39.	PLUNGED	Pushed firmly into a container
40.	PRECAUTION	Action taken to protect against harm
41.	PRECIOUS	Much loved and valued
42.	PROWL	Move around in a sneaky way
43.	RUCKSACK	Backpack
44.	SALON	Elegant room in a private home
45.	SHAWL	Piece of fabric worn over the shoulders
46.	SKIPPED	Chose to not go to an activity
47.	SOLID	Strong; firm
48.	SPROUT	Grow quickly
49.	STAMMERING	Speaking with many pauses and repetitions
50.	STENCH	Foul, disgusting smell
51.	STOW	Put something away for future use

Letters From Rifka Vocabulary Word List

No.	Word	Clue/Definition
52.	STUBBORN	Willful; not cooperative
53.	TEMPEST	Severe storm with strong winds and rain
54.	TILTED	Slanted; leaning at an angle
55.	TORMENTED	Inflicted pain or discomfort
56.	TOUSLE	Tangle or mess up hair
57.	WARD	Hospital room for several patients
58.	WITS	Intelligence; common sense

www.ingramcontent.com/pod-product-compliance
Lightning Source LLC
Chambersburg PA
CBHW051408070526
44584CB00023B/3336